DOUGLAS A. HILL
Formerly Principal Lecturer in Geography
Borough Road College, Isleworth

Northern Ireland

CONTENTS

Acknowledgements *p. 2*
1 The North-East Coastlands *p. 3*
2 The Mourne Country *p. 17*
3 Lough Neagh and the Armagh Fruitlands *p. 23*
4 Co. Fermanagh and the South-West *p. 29*
5 Londonderry *p. 35*
6 Ballymena *p. 39*
7 Belfast *p. 44*
8 Industries – old and new *p. 55*
9 Farming *p. 62*
10 The People – their origins and customs *p. 71*
Colour maps A-D are between pages 36 and 37

CAMBRIDGE UNIVERSITY PRESS
CAMBRIDGE
LONDON · NEW YORK · MELBOURNE

Published by the Syndics of the Cambridge University Press
The Pitt Building, Trumpington Street, Cambridge CB2 1RP
Bentley House, 200 Euston Road, London NW1 2DB
32 East 57th Street, New York, NY 10022, USA
296 Beaconsfield Parade, Middle Park, Melbourne 3206, Australia

© Cambridge University Press 1974

ISBN 0 521 20027 X

First published 1974
Reprinted with corrections 1978

Filmset in Great Britain by Keyspools Ltd, Golborne, Lancashire
Printed in Great Britain at the University Press, Cambridge

Geography of the British Isles Series

Greater London   W. S. DANCER AND A. V. HARDY
North West England   W. E. MARSDEN
Yorkshire and North Lincolnshire   H. TOLLEY AND K. ORRELL
South-East England   H. J. SAVORY
The British Isles   A. V. HARDY
North East England   J. E. WALTHAM AND W. D. HOLMES
The West Midlands   C. PRITCHARD
South West England   H. D. BLACK

ACKNOWLEDGEMENTS

The author wishes to acknowledge the help given by Mr M. Cox and Mr T. McVeigh with the material for the sample farms and to the farmers without whose co-operation this part of the work would have been impossible.

Thanks are due to Professor Emrys Jones, Mr D. George and Mr A. V. Hardy for reading the manuscript and offering many valuable suggestions.

For permission to reproduce maps, diagrams and photographs thanks are due to Mr L. H. Houston and to the Ulster Tourist Board for Figs. 13, 14, 16, 31, 35, 36, 41, 53, 58, 59 and 93; to the Government Information Offices for Figs. 77 and 89; to Messrs R. J. Anderson & Co. for Figs. 79, 85 and 91; to Fruitfield Preserves Ltd for Figs. 44 and 45; to Messrs Harland & Wolff for Fig. 82; to Geographical Association of Northern Ireland for Figs. 33, 40 and 102; to Messrs Aerofilms for Figs. 2, 23, 39, 57, 62, 75, 76, 78, 80 and 90; to Ordnance Survey of Northern Ireland for Colour Maps A, B, C and D, and Figs. 12, 47, 55, 56, 96, 97, 99, 100, 101, 102; to *Belfast Telegraph* for Figs. 9 and 88; to the Central Office of Information for Fig. 84.

The author worked in the Friends' School, Lisburn and Queen's University, Belfast for 20 years and made many contributions to geographical research and teaching including the Land Utilisation Survey.

1 | THE NORTH-EAST COASTLANDS

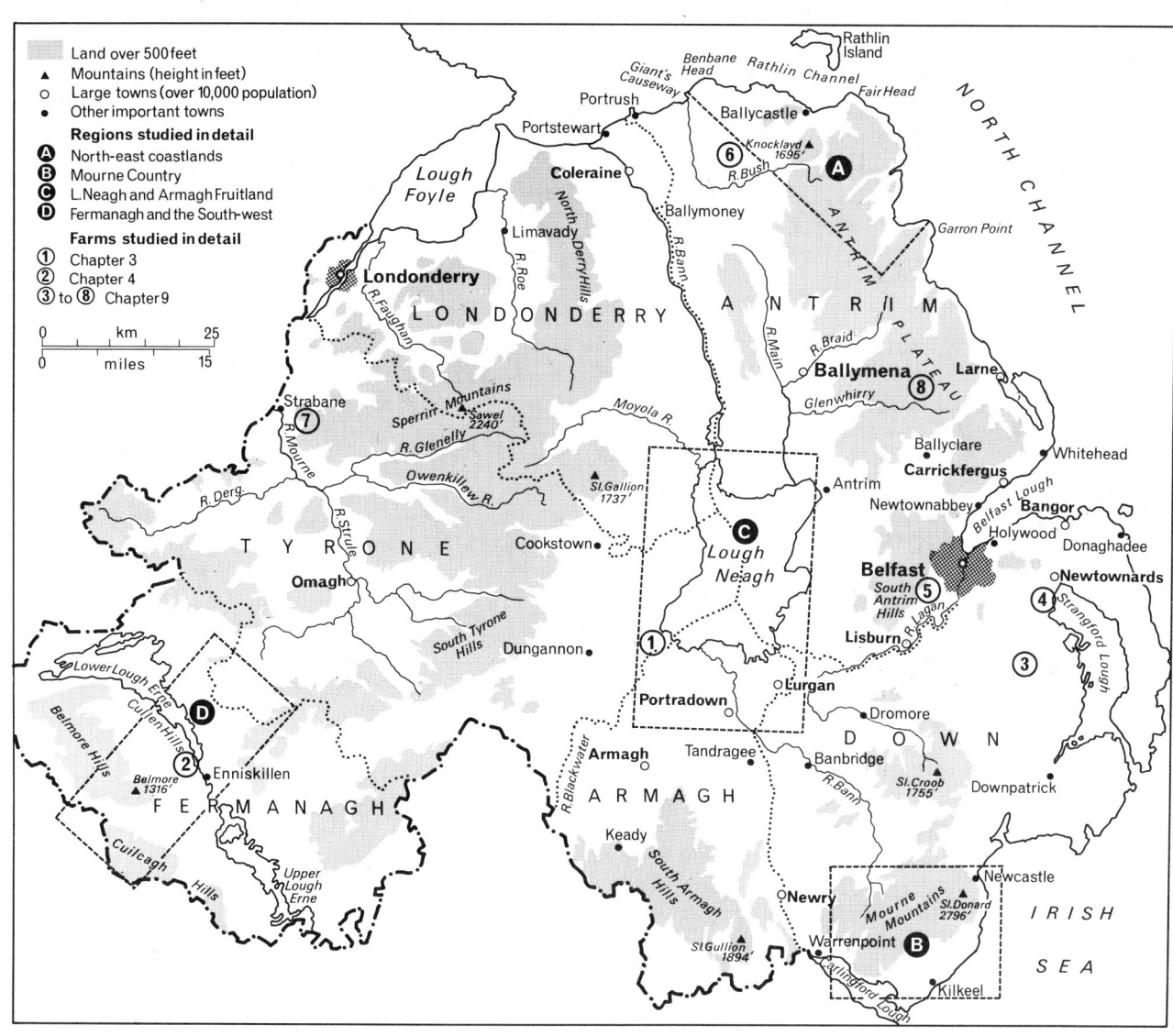

1. Reference map of N. Ireland

Standing boldly out into the North Channel is Fair Head, the most north-easterly headland of Ireland. Across the North Channel lies the peninsula of Kintyre, about 14 miles (22.5 km) away whilst further to the west are the islands of Islay and Mull in the Inner Hebrides. Much nearer, about 4 miles (6.4 km) across the Rathlin Channel, is Rathlin Island. Either way from Fair Head runs a coastline of great headlands and deep bays which together form areas of great natural charm. Southwards along the east coast is the 'Glen Country' which

3

2. An aerial view of Glenariff looking north-east from point X in Colour Map A. Compare the picture and the map and notice how deeply cut the glen is

centres around Cushendall. To the westward for some 15 to 20 miles (24–32 km), bay and headland succeed each other to end in the Giant's Causeway which overlooks the dune-choked bay around the mouth of the river Bush. Seaside towns, Ballycastle, Portballantrae and Portrush, nestle in the bays and provide for many tourists.

The Glen Country

The view shown in Fig. 2 is looking north-east from point X on Colour map A. The exercises on the map (on p. 16) will help you to read the picture which is of Glenariff, one of the nine glens of Antrim. In the distance can be seen the sea and beyond, a part of Scotland. At its seaward end, the glen has the shape of a broad U with steep sides and high hills beyond.

The great valley was shaped by a tongue of ice which probably moved up from the direction of the sea. As the ice melted it left a large lake which could only disappear when the melting of the ice allowed the water to escape from the lower end to the sea. Now all that is left is a small meandering river – a misfit in this very large valley.

At the upper end nearer to X, the valley becomes very narrow and forms a gorge where the river falls over the edge of the plateau whilst at X the river is on the plateau and is a narrow mountain stream.

Whilst the ice blocked the seaward end of Glenariff, the lake received water from the melting ice and grew larger until it overflowed the watershed in the mountains near Loughnafanogy, and has left behind a deeply cut valley

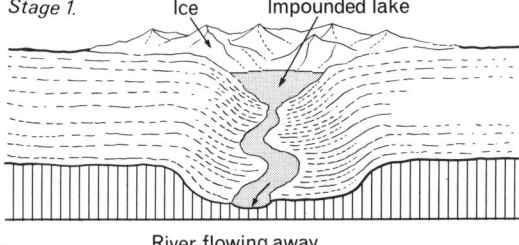
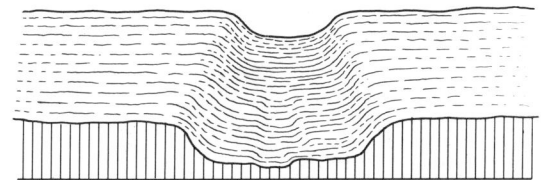

Stage 1. Ice — Impounded lake
River flowing away from the ice edge and cutting a valley as it flowed.

Stage 2. The ice has melted; river has disappeared for lack of water from the melting ice. The valley is left dry and is called an 'overflow channel.'

3. Stages in the development of an 'overflow channel'

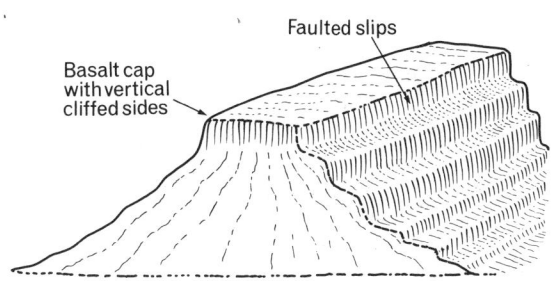

4. Lurigethan: a mountain spur between Glenariff and Glen Ballyemon

Basalt cap with vertical cliffed sides — Faulted slips

5. Ess-na-Croob Falls in Glenariff

marking the old watercourse (Fig. 3). Such a valley is called an 'overflow' channel because it took the overflow of water from the lake.

Between the glens great spurs of the plateau jut out towards the sea. Find Lurigethan on Colour Map A; it lies between Glenariff and Glen Ballyemon. Usually these spurs have flat tops and very steep, stepped sides (Fig. 4). Their shape is influenced by the rock formations and the faults, as the diagram shows.

The glens fall into three parts: (*a*) the broad lower part with a flat floor covered with thick alluvium, (*b*) the steep gorge (400–800′, 122–244 m) where the river falls over the edge of the plateau, and (*c*) the upper mountain valley on the plateau. A fine waterfall, of which there are many in the steep gorge section, is shown in Fig. 5. The various layers of basalt

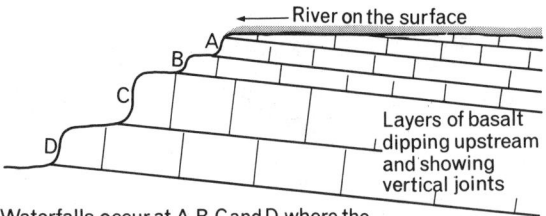

Waterfalls occur at A, B, C and D where the river flows over the edges of the basalt layers

6. The development of a waterfall

7. Pot-holes being formed in the bed of the Glenariff river gorge

8. The south side of Glenariff and part of the flat river floor

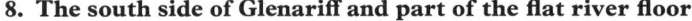

rock explain the position of the waterfalls in the gorge (Fig. 6). As the rushing water flows over the rock bed it moves boulders along and often they develop a circular motion, so carving out pot-holes (Fig. 7).

A part of the lower glen is shown in Fig. 8. The ridges on the steep slope mark the different layers in the rock structure whilst the flat floor is often flooded from the meandering Glenariff river. As Colour Map A shows, the river has been straightened artificially to increase the gradient and the speed of flow, and thus reduce the amount of flooding.

The coastline has many points of interest. Find Garron Point on Colour Map A and study it in the picture (Fig. 9). Compare Fig. 10 with the picture at A. Where do the faults lie in the picture? Their effect is to form (a) the high plateau, (b) the steep cliffs, and (c) the low plateau. In the cliffs the picture shows a part which is white and a part black. The colours correspond to the underlying chalk rock and a thick overlying sheet of basalt – solidified lava which covers so much of Co. Antrim, and forms the steep black cliffs of the coastline.

9. Garron Point. The dark basalt and white chalk cliffs contrast clearly

Below the cliffs, a broad bench upon which the road runs, stretches all along the coast. In Fig. 11 the bench is shown at (d). Such a bench is called a 'raised beach', that is, one that used to be washed by the sea but is now lifted above it. In Co. Antrim it is usually 15/25 ft (4.6/7.6 m) above the present sea-level and may be made of sand and pebbles or it may be a platform eroded out of the solid rocks. At Garron Point it is the latter but at the mouth of Glenariff it is the former.

Lands, like Northern Ireland, which were covered with thick ice during the Great Ice Age, were crushed downwards by its weight. When the ice melted and the weight was removed, the land was uplifted so that changes occurred in the relative height of the land and the sea. The formation of raised beaches was one result of these changes.

In the centre of Fig. 8 several isolated houses are seen at intervals along the road. These are the more modern farmsteads and show that most present-day farms surround the house and farmstead. The picture also shows that the fields are arranged in strips from the river to the top of the hills. Each strip stretches

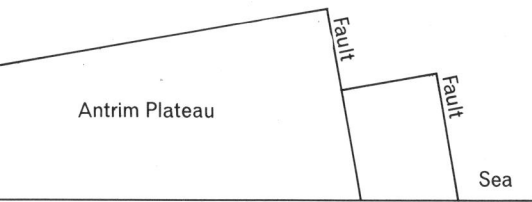

10. Formation of cliffs in Antrim. Compare with the picture (Fig. 9). The cliff-edge of the plateau is often marked by one or more faults, as shown in the diagram. The effect of these can be seen in the picture in (a) the high plateau top, (b) the steep cliffs, and (c) the low plateau on which the large school is situated

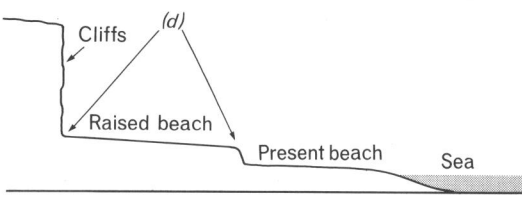

11. A raised beach

7

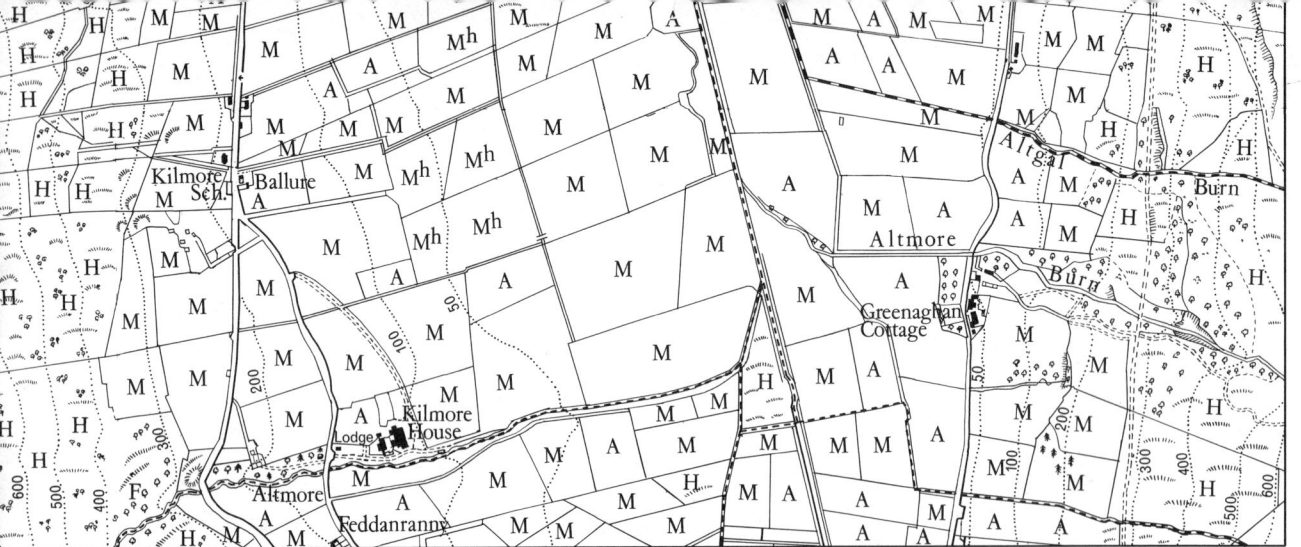

Key   A Land in crops   M Land under grass   H Rough hill land and peat   F Woodland
12. Land use in the Glenariff river valley (based on O.S. map, by permission)

across all qualities of land, from the low-lying meadows near the river to the drier, better land around the farmstead and then on to the rough mountain pasture and peat on the higher mountains. From the map (Fig. 12) work out the use of the land in each of these areas – the river lowland, around the farm and on the hills.

The mountain provides the peat which has been used for fuel for a very long time. Today it is being replaced by electricity which has come to the glens fairly recently, bringing power to each farm for both domestic and farming purposes. Modern domestic appliances and farm machines can now be used.

Stock farming is the most important farming enterprise. Farms vary in size, often with the quality of the land. Heavy rainfall, poor drainage in the lower part of the valley and large amounts of steep and mountainous land make crop growing difficult. Black-faced mountain sheep are kept on the higher rough grazing. Galloway cattle also graze the higher lands. Small herds of dairy cattle and bullocks are usual on the lower lands.

The North Coast
Much of this coastline from the Giant's Causeway to White Park Bay belongs to the National Trust and a fine coastal walk has been made throughout the Causeway and then on to White Park Bay and Ballintoy.

Sand dunes have formed in each of the bays. In the rear of the cold fronts, winds from the north-west blow strongly across the wide expanse of ocean offshore. They gather the beach sands and blow them towards the south-east side of the bays where they accumulate, often covering the raised beaches which lie behind the present shore-line. The dunes make excellent golf courses, as at Portrush and Ballycastle (Fig. 13).

All along the northern coast the rock layers have been tilted so that the steep edge lies along the coast and the beds dip inland. The land increases in height as the coast is approached and cliffs of 300 ft (91.4 m) in the Giant's Causeway and 600 ft (182.8 m) in Fair Head form bold headlands.

The high Causeway cliffs surrounding Benbane Head show the formation of the basalt rocks most clearly (Fig. 14). The lavas flowed out at different times and formed the layers of basalt. Often there was a long period of time between one flow and the next so that the surface of the lower flow was weakened and often eroded off before the next one poured out upon it. Fig. 14 shows how the land is built layer by layer. The coastal cliffs are often vertical as the basalt is jointed in this direction and columns break away leaving large screes down the face of the cliffs.

The Giant's Causeway is of great interest

13. Golf course on the dunes at Portrush

14. The Giant's Causeway, showing the vertical cliffs and the layers of basalt

15. A vertical picture showing the cross-section of the basalt columns

16. The basalt columns

10

because the jointing caused the basalt, as it cooled, to form long columns which are usually hexagonal in shape (Fig. 15). There were three major outpourings of lava, of which two are well shown in the Giant's Causeway. Little of the most recent flow remains as severe erosion has removed most of it but much of the second flow remains. As it cooled, it formed the great columns shown in Fig. 16, which give to the Causeway its character.

Before the outpouring of this middle basalt, there was a long quiet period and the surface of the earlier and lower basalt layer was exposed to the weather for a long time. Probably, too, at that time the weather over Northern Ireland was very hot and moist, so creating ideal conditions for extensive chemical weathering such as that which is experienced in equatorial regions today. As a result of these conditions the top twenty feet (6 m) of lower basalt has decayed to form a bright red band of laterite containing both iron ore and bauxite. In places the weathering process is not complete and the form of the columns can still be seen, as shown in Fig. 17a. These are called 'Giant's Eyes' locally. The stages in their formation are illustrated in Fig. 17b.

All along this coast there are many features which have been formed by the erosive power of the sea. Fig. 18 shows one of these. The rocks have been planed off by the waves to form a low platform whilst the harder pieces have been left and stand up as 'stacks'.

White Park Bay and Ballintoy Harbour

At the eastern end of the Giant's Causeway a fault cuts through the rocks from the north-west to south-east. This fault has the effect of bringing the chalk which underlies the basalt to the surface around White Park Bay (Fig. 19). The basalt has been removed by erosion from a wide coastal stretch; the coast is lower (50/100′, 15.2/30.5 m) much less rugged and flanked by chalk cliffs. The edge of the basalt lies some distance inland and forms a steep scarp above the chalk plateau.

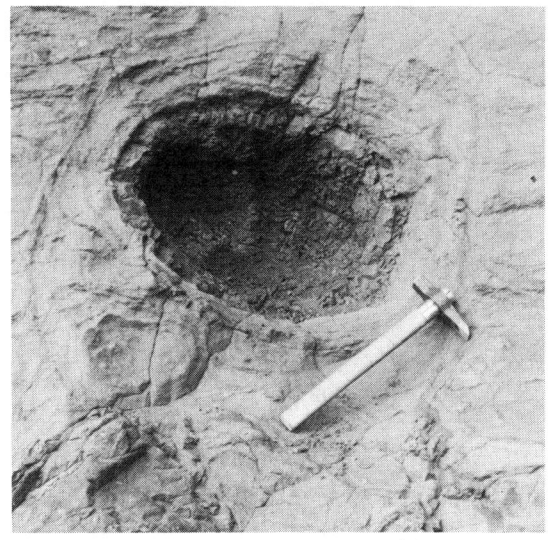

17a

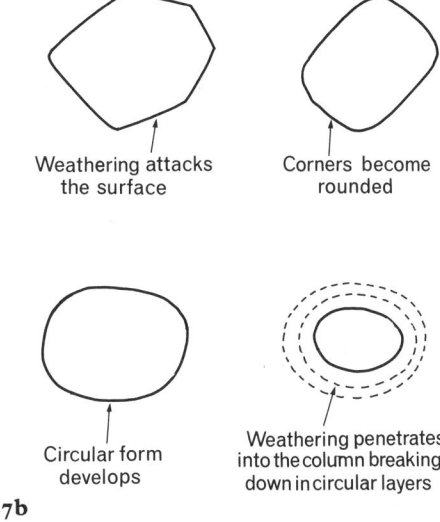

17b

17. These 'Giant's Eyes' mark parts of the basalt which have not fully decayed into laterite. The basalt decays in layers. If this occurs around the hexagonal columns, the circular form will develop. The photograph shows a very large one which has decayed quite markedly but all around it other 'Giant's Eyes' can also be seen in formation

White Park Bay belongs to the National Trust and is preserved from building development. Near its western end and where it is protected by Gid Point, is the small fishing harbour of Port Braddan, noted for its salmon and lobsters. At the eastern end upon the great sand dunes is an earthwork dating from the New Stone Age, showing that people have lived along these coasts for a very long time. Today the bay attracts many tourists and in its midst stands a Youth Hostel.

With so much basalt, there must have been many volcanoes through which the lavas came to the surface. The remains of these volcanoes are usually hidden under the basalt cover but two come to the surface just east of White Park Bay. Fig. 20 shows the solidified lava in the neck of one of these. The white chalk through which the lavas moved upwards can be seen all around it. Nearby are beds of tuffs formed from the volcanic ash, whilst dykes (Fig. 21) often occur. The diagrams in Fig. 22 suggest how these features may have been formed.

Ballycastle Bay from Kinbane Head to Fair Head
Kinbane Head which forms the western arm of the bay, rises to about 300 ft (91.4 m). Fair Head on the east is over 600 ft (182.6 m) with the upper 300 ft (91.4 m) as a vertical cliff. Kinbane Head is composed of chalk whereas Fair Head marks the seaward end of a large sill of dolerite.

The sill (Fig. 23) was in the first place enclosed within the Carboniferous rocks. Erosion, especially during the Great Ice Age,

18. **Giant's Causeway: a wave-cut rock platform and stack**

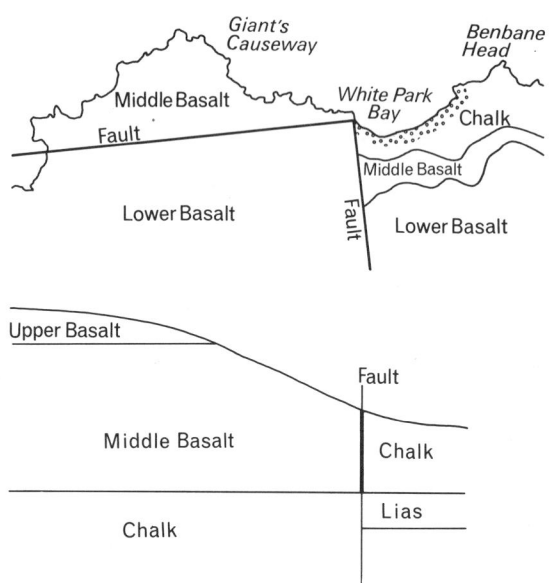

19. **Sketch-map and section showing the coast at White Park Bay**

20. **A volcanic neck at Ballintoy Harbour**

has removed the top layer of the Carboniferous rocks and the sill now forms the surface of Fair Head. Upon it there are many glacial features including roches moutonnées and the rock basin lakes, Lough Doo and Lough na Crannog (Fig. 23).

The dolerite, like most basalts, forms large columns as it cools. These columns are gradually weakened along their joints by weathering and many have fallen seawards to form an enormous pile of scree around the base of the cliff (Fig. 23).

Between these two headlands is Ballycastle Bay which is some five miles wide from east to west and about two miles north to south.

21. A dyke at Ballintoy Harbour

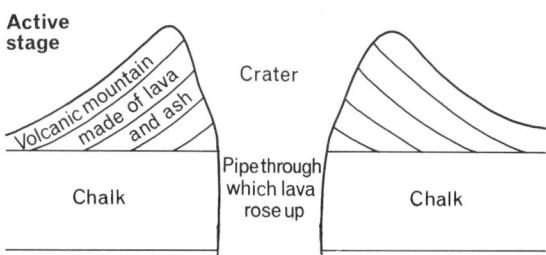

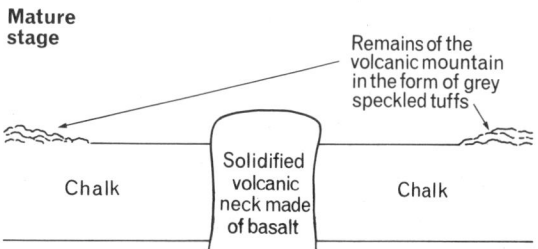

22. Formation of a volcanic neck, tuffs, etc.

23. Fair Head, showing vertical cliff, scree and glacially eroded surface

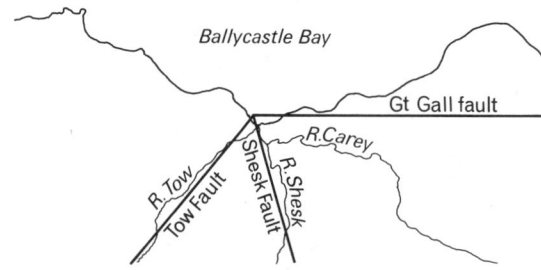

24. Formation of Ballycastle Bay

25. Coastal cliffs at Ballycastle Bay, showing thick sandstones and thin beds of shale and coal

The centre of the bay occurs where three faults meet (Fig. 24) so causing subsidence at a point of structural weakness. The faults have moved the strata vertically so that a great variety of rocks occur at the surface in a small area. For instance, to the west of the Tow fault the basalt comes to the surface at sea-level, but on Knocklayd to the east its base lies 700 ft (213.4 m) above sea-level. Both the Tow and Shesk faults are followed by valleys which have been fashioned by the movement of ice in the Great Ice Age. Now each is occupied by a river and these converge in Ballycastle to enter the sea as a single stream – the river Margy.

Like White Park Bay, the south-eastern part of the bay is choked with large dunes, along the seaward side of which is a sandy strand over one mile (1.6 km) in length. Between the eastern end of the dunes and Fair Head, the Carboniferous Limestone series forms the coastal cliffs (Fig. 25). The more massive sandstones separate the narrower layers of coal and shale. Mining is no longer carried on but all along the coast are adits (Fig. 26) through which the coal was mined in the eighteenth century for shipment, especially to Dublin.

Below these cliffs at about 20 ft (6 m) above present sea-level is an old raised shore-line upon which is built the coastal road. Seawards from this and at present sea-level, is a wide rock platform which is being eroded by the sea. As not all the rocks erode at the same rate, or indeed in the same way, this rock platform shows many erosional features. Fig. 27 shows how a hard dyke (North Star Dyke) of andesite – a type of basalt – has resisted the work of the waves and stands higher than the surrounding platform. Fig. 28 shows a band of limestone amongst the sandstones; it is fretted into small clints and grykes whereas the sandstones below are devoid of such formations. This difference is due to the fact that limestone dissolves in water and the sandstones do not.

26. Mining adit, Ballycastle Bay, near North Star Dyke

27. North Star Dyke

28. Limestone on Ballycastle marine platform fretted by dissolution in sea-water

Questions on Colour Map A

1. Name and give the heights of the mountain summits shown on the map.

Name the two glens shown on the map.

2. Make a tracing of the land over 1000 ft high. Estimate the area of this land in comparison with the whole.

3. Draw a section from Limerick Point through the summit of Lurigethan to Crockalough. This section shows theee main physical features of the area. Name them.

4. You can study the physical geography of Glenariff by working the following exercises:

(*a*) Draw a section along the Glenariff river from the source of the Inver River to the mouth at Waterfoot. Divide this section into three parts: the mountain river over 900′, the gorge, 300′–900′ and the valley below 300′. Measure the length of each part and compare them.

(*b*) Draw three cross-sections: (i) from Lurigethan to Knockore; (ii) Crockalough to Crockravar; (iii) Glenariff Lodge to Loughracurry. How do these sections differ in shape and what do the differences tell about the shape of the glen?

2 | THE MOURNE COUNTRY

The Mourne country is situated in the south-east part of County Down with the seaside town of Newcastle to the north-east and Rostrevor to the south-west. For 15 miles (24.4 km) between these two resorts stretch the Mourne Mountains which rise gradually towards the north-east where they overlook the Irish Sea in the highest peak – Slieve Donard (2796', 860 m). South-east of the mountains lies the Mourne Plain. It is almost enclosed between the mountains and the sea, access only being possible by the narrow coastal passes at each end and by one pass (the Spelga Pass) over the mountains themselves.

Co. Down is mostly composed of slates and grits similar in age to those found in the Scottish Uplands. In many quarries along the coast and elsewhere, the beds of slate and grit can be seen either standing vertically or at a sharp angle. Much severe contortion must have taken place at the time of the formation of the Mourne Mountains to move them from the horizontal position in which they were originally laid down. Fig. 29 shows the strata looked at from above. It was taken along the coast at Annalong and an igneous dyke can be seen running across the beds.

The Mourne Mountains are made of several types of granite – a rock which was intruded into the strata, so causing the layers to bend upwards. Fig. 30 shows the stages by which the Mourne Mountains were made. Most of the slate covering the granite has been eroded off but here and there, as on Finlieve or Slieve Muck, it still remains on the summits. Elsewhere the granite comes to the surface and forms a series of peaks (Fig. 31).

Ice covered the Mourne Mountains during the Great Ice Age. Such peaks as Slieve Donard and Slieve Commedagh show the smooth, rounded form which suggests they were completely covered by the ice. Slieve Bernagh has a summit of large irregular columns which suggests that it stood above the ice and was subject to shattering by frost action just above the ice cover. Often the ice stripped the granite off along the joints, peeling it like an onion, and as a result of the erosion large and small boulders are strewn everywhere. One very large one – the Cloughmore Stone – lies above Rostrevor. On the northern slopes of the mountains are a few small cirques where local glaciers probably formed. Most of the soil was removed by the ice and as the granite is so hard a new layer of soil has not had time to form.

29. Annalong, Co. Down, looking down vertically at the strata running from top to bottom. Note the igneous dyke running across the picture

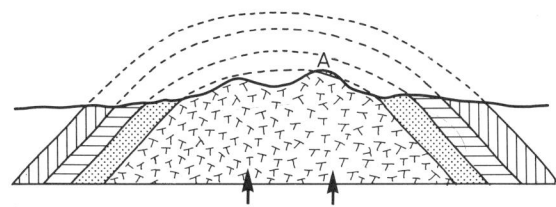

Granite, an igneous rock, was pushed up from the interior of the Earth and bent the layers of slates and shale upwards above it into a dome.
Erosion has worn the top of the dome away, leaving a few fragments of slate and shale on the mountain summits (A) but usually exposing the granite. The slates and shales now form upright or steeply sloping layers all around the granite.

Granite   Slates and shales   Eroded away

30. Formation of the Mourne Mountains

31. Mourne Peaks (granite) in background, lowland (boulder clay) with drumlins in foreground

Except for a few small patches, as in Castle Bog, very little peat has accumulated.

The mountains present a very barren appearance relieved only by heather, sparse mountain grasses and whin. Granite boulders – often white and naked – stand out amongst these. Only on the flanks where some drift material occurs, near Newcastle and at Rostrevor, have any large areas of woodland been planted.

The ice, which has so denuded the mountains and has opened up the valleys into typical U-valleys (e.g. Silent Valley), has covered the surrounding lowlands with deposits of sand, stones, and boulder clay.

To the north of the mountains lie the boulder clays in which moving ice has fashioned many drumlins (Fig. 31). A drumlin is a small hill composed of boulder clay. Sometimes it has a solid rock core. It is long and narrow with one steep end (the stoss end) and a more gentle slope at the other end – the two forming the long axis (Fig. 32). These hills influence the use of the land. Roads twine themselves around them. Farmsteads are often situated near the summit or on the flanks. Field shapes are

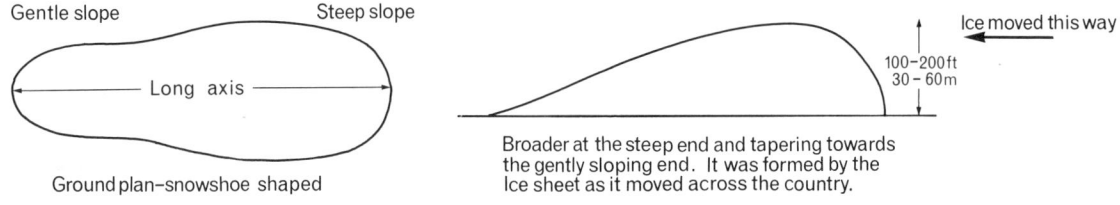

32. Formation of drumlins. The drumlin is broader at the steep end and tapers towards the gently sloping end. It was formed by the ice sheet as this moved across country

18

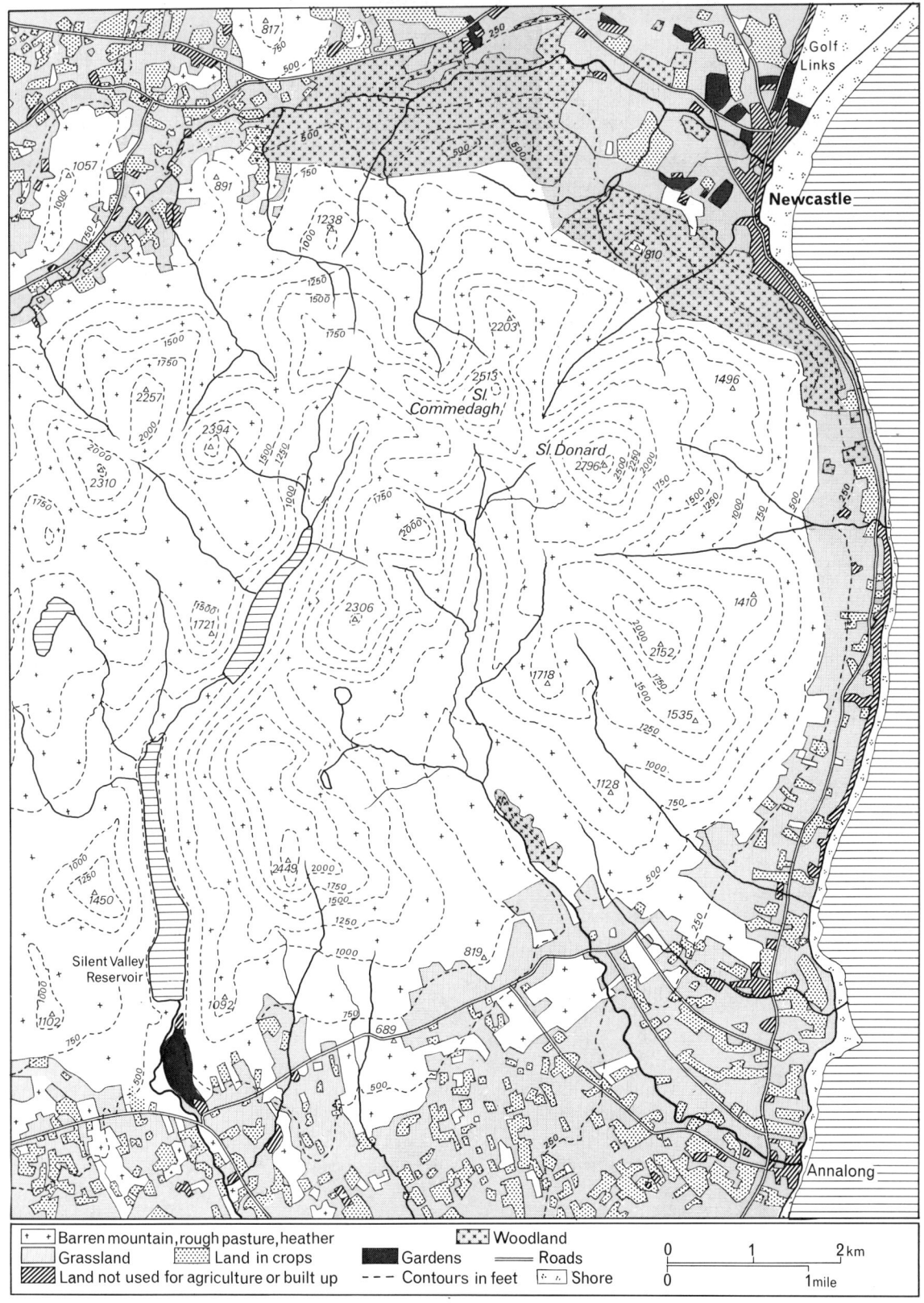

33. Land-use map of part of the Mournes (based on L.U.S. map, by permission)

34. Deer's Meadow Reservoir

35. Mourne Plain, showing a single gate-post stone, stone walls and small farmstead

adapted to the form of the hill with hedges following the long and short axes.

Around Kilkeel, moraines and sandy mounds give the countryside its main features. These were formed where small glaciers moved out from the mountains and melted on reaching the lowland. At the point of melting a semi-circular moraine was formed around the mouth of the mountain valleys.

It is only along the coast on the wide raised beach that level land occurs. The rivers which flow from the mountains across the plain to the sea have cut their valleys very deeply in the loose drifts and flow in deep gorges. Many have cut through the drifts to the solid rock beneath and are impeded by waterfalls and rapids.

The land-use map (Fig. 33) suggests ways in which man has been able to live in this area. The mountains offer three opportunities: they are wild and beautiful and so attract tourists; they have a very high average rainfall (over 100" or 254 cm, in places) and so provide water for Belfast and other towns and villages (Fig. 34); granite is a hard and valuable rock so quarries are frequent and stone-dressing is done in the small towns like Annalong. For the farmer, the mountains are a poor land, the chief usage being the rearing of Mourne grey-faced sheep.

The foreground of Fig. 35 shows part of the drift-covered plain around the base of the mountains. The farmsteads are scattered evenly over the land and their large white gate-posts, made of boulders, are a marked feature of the landscape. Nearer the mountains these white posts are often replaced by one long, upright granite stone.

These lands have not been easy to farm as they are full of stones and boulders. A first stage in using the land was to remove them, and many have been used in the building of stone walls around the fields, the farm houses and other buildings.

By very hard work and the use of seaweed as manure, a moderately good, rather light and stony soil has been produced. Herds of a few cattle are kept on most farms but much of the land is used for potatoes. These are exported from Kilkeel to South Wales. The protection from northerly winds provided by the mountains makes it possible to plant potatoes early in the spring. Difficulties have arisen with the potato crop owing to a serious attack by eelworms. There is no cure except to stop growing potatoes for seven or more years. Other crops, including oats, are much less important. Sheep are numerous using both mountain and lowland pastures.

The farms are small, often less than 20 acres (8 hectares). It is not easy to make a good living

36. Mending the fishing nets at Annalong. The picture also shows a disused corn mill, the use of granite blocks in the older buildings and the harbour wall, and the open inshore fishing boats

from them. Although tractors and other machinery are used, hand methods such as the drilling fiddle and the scythe have not completely died out. Many farmers, too, turn to the sea and fish the inshore waters for herring and lobster (Fig. 36).

Finally the coast itself offers opportunities. At Kilkeel and Annalong are fishing fleets with their larger boats. These can travel farther, catching herring, plaice, haddock and cod. Extensive improvements have been made to Kilkeel harbour providing for 60 modern fishing boats. A slipway for maintenance and new factories to process fish are being built. Golf on the dunes at Newcastle and yachting in Carlingford Lough are popular pastimes.

Thus from mountain, plain and sea the people draw their living. Few people live in the mountains, but the plain is more densely populated. Many of its people are farmers, but others must look to tourism, forestry, granite working, fishing and the newer light industries for their livelihood. Even so there is not enough work and many must go out of the area to find work either by daily commuting or by long-term emigration. There is often great reluctance to take the latter course, so strong are family ties.

Questions on Colour Map B

1. On the map is shown the highest peak in the Mourne Mountains. What is the name and height of this peak?

2. What does the map show about the use of the water of the Kilkeel river? How is this done? Find out all you can about the scheme which uses the water of this river.

3. Draw a simple sketch-map which will divide the area of the map into physical regions. What differences do you notice between them?

4. At what height do the settlements cease? Does the map suggest a reason?

5. Does the map suggest any reason for the position of Kilkeel?

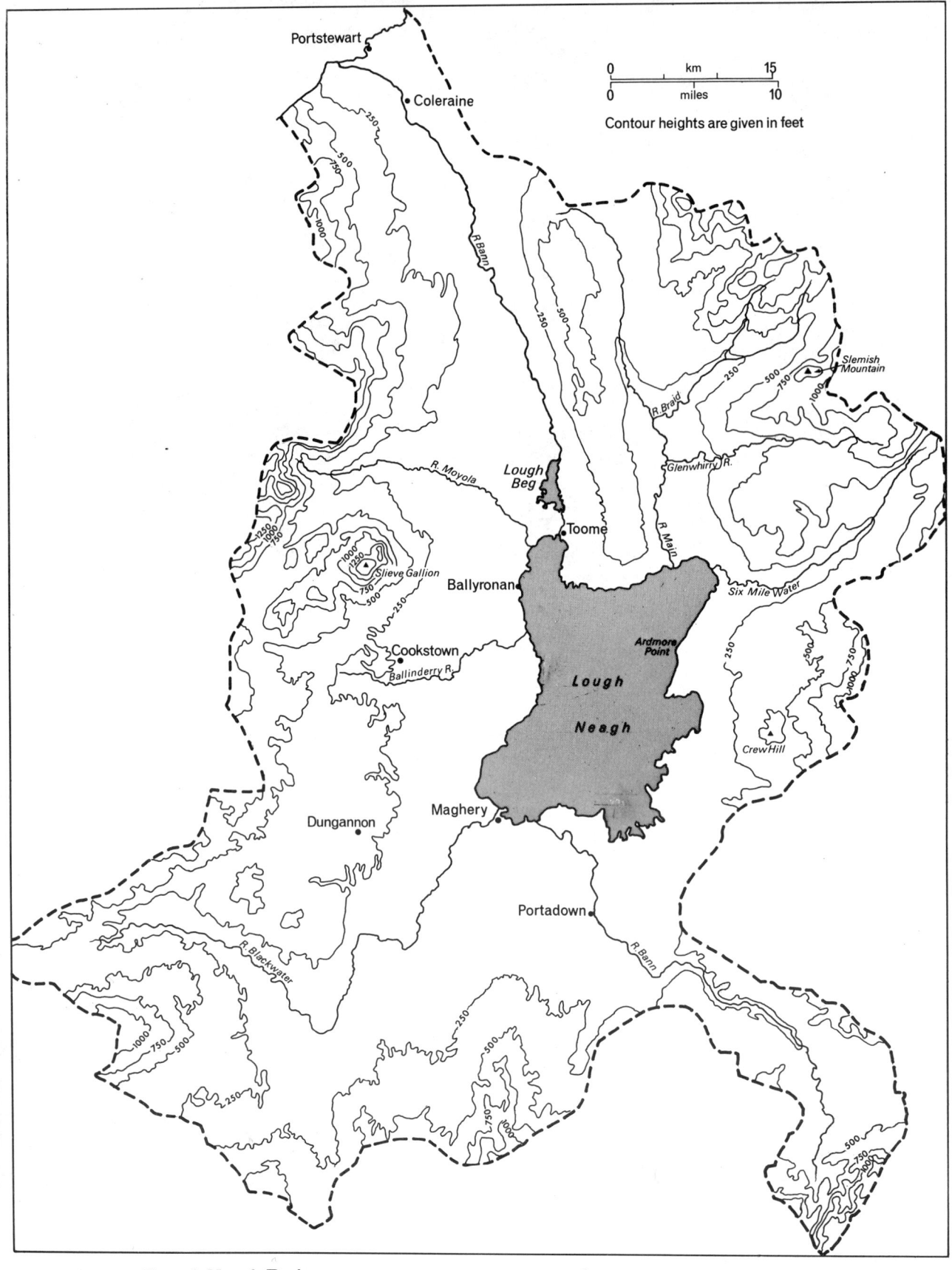

37. Lough Neagh Basin

3 | LOUGH NEAGH AND THE ARMAGH FRUITLANDS

The answers to the exercises (see p. 28) on the map (Fig. 37) will tell you about the size of Lough Neagh and the important place it has in the drainage system of Northern Ireland.

To the east of Lough Neagh the land rises gradually to the Antrim Hills and in the west to the Sperrin Mountains and the uplands of Co. Tyrone. The Lough lies in a shallow basin formed by the crossing of two fault lines (Fig. 38). The lowlands have been covered with glacial drifts and it is these which provide the physical features of the surrounding shorelands. To the east these drifts are usually heavy boulder clay with some sandy mounds but few drumlins. They tend to be flat, often very wet and even waterlogged. They are used for permanent pasture which supports dairy herds supplying milk to Belfast and small herds of bullocks. This flat area near to Belfast provides a suitable site for the chief airport at Aldergrove.

The western side of the Lough is much more hummocky, with many sandy glacial mounds. These tend to produce rather lighter soils. Farms on this side of the Lough are small, often under 30 acres (12 ha). They support mixed husbandry with bullocks, pigs and poultry as the chief livestock.

To the south of the Lough are the wet lowlands at the mouths of the rivers Bann and Blackwater. Drainage works help to prevent waterlogging and flooding and so allow pastures to occupy large areas but extensive peat bogs occur, especially around the mouth of the river Blackwater.

Settlements lie back from the lake shore on the higher ground, the largest being the route centres and bridging points (e.g. Portadown, Antrim, Magherafelt and Toome). Fishing for eels and pollen has several centres around the shores, the largest being Toome where a series of eel traps cross the river Bann just below the lake (Fig. 39).

Fig. 40 shows a part of the Land Utilisation (L.U.S.) Map of the area south of Lough

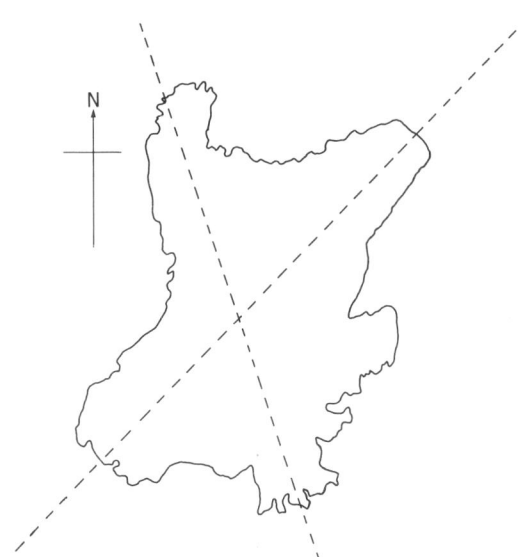

38. Lough Neagh, showing the general direction of the fault lines and their influence on the shape of the Lough

39. Eel traps at Toome across the river Lower Bann

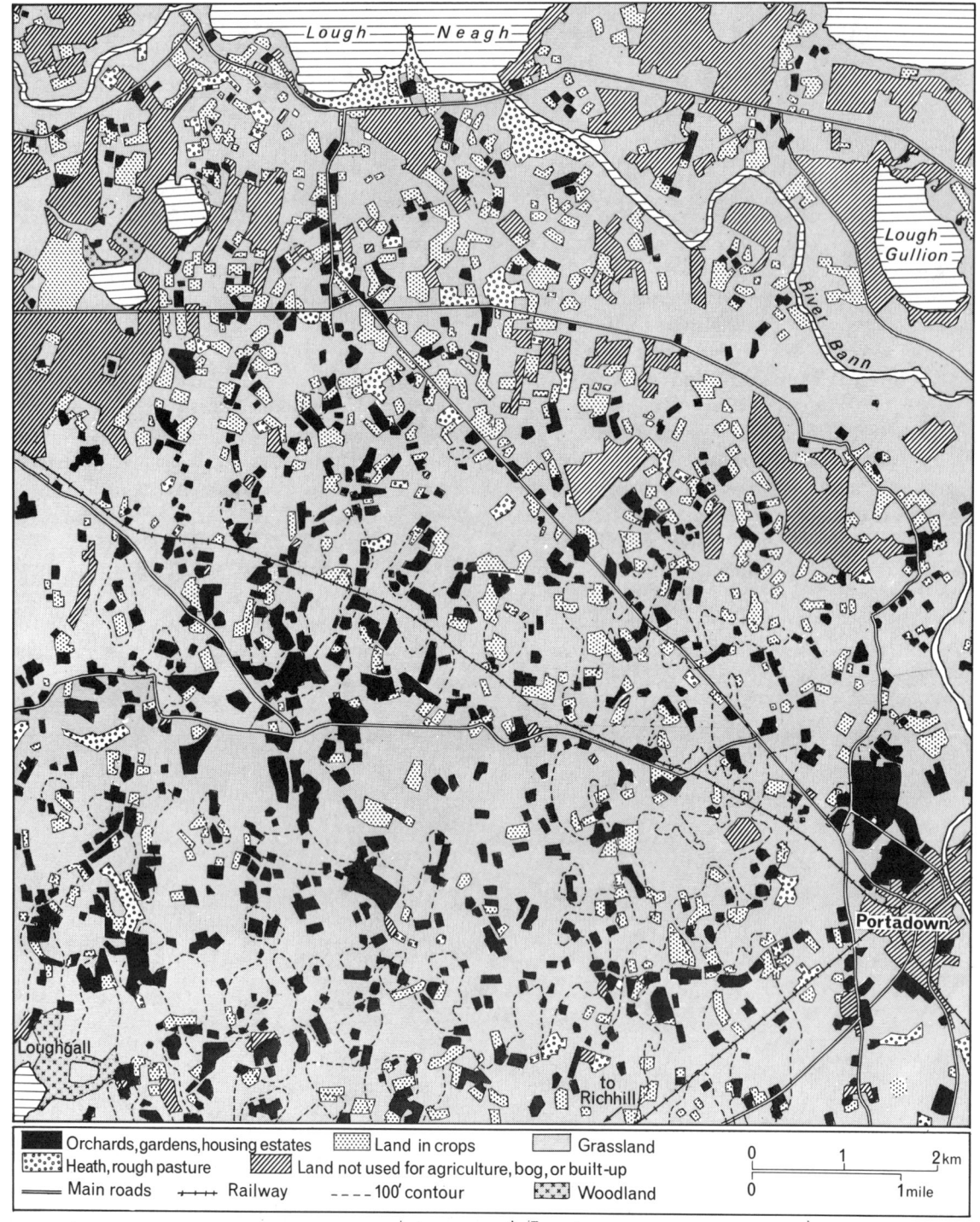

40. Land-use map of part of the Armagh fruitlands (based on L.U.S. map, by permission)

41. Cutting peat. Note the marks on the peatface where sods have been cut and the shape of the spade, the two sides of which the man is holding. A special long barrow is used

Neagh. Study the map and then answer the questions upon it at the end of the chapter (p. 28).

Although the whole area from Lough Neagh in the north to Armagh in the south-west is lowland, it is an area of contrasting scenery. Near the shores of Lough Neagh the land is very low-lying and extensive areas of peat occur. Drainage is the chief problem in the usage of these lake shorelands and extensive flooding often occurs. The cutting of peat (Fig. 41) for fuel and other purposes has reduced the area of bog. Given suitable drainage the peaty soils are valuable for potatoes, rhubarb, strawberries and some root crops.

Scattered amongst the peat bogs are mounds of higher land. These are usually drumlins and on them farms are sited. Many are very small. They usually support herds of Ayrshire and Shorthorn cattle for milk. Poultry are found on almost all farms. Most of the land is in pasture to feed the cattle but some kale and oats are grown. These are not easy lands to farm. The acid, heavy soils require artificial drainage to prevent waterlogging. Modernisation in the form of tractors and the use of electricity has come to many of the farms but horses and donkeys are still used in some places.

Lying to the south of the lake shore area is the chief fruit-farming district in Northern Ireland. Like so many of the lowlands, ice covered it during the Great Ice Age and left behind a mixture of drifts with sand towards the east but elsewhere mostly boulder clay. This part of Co. Armagh forms part of the great drumlin belt which stretches from the Irish Sea to Donegal Bay (see Fig. 32 and page 18 for the formation of the drumlins).

The drumlins lie in lines, developed parallel to the flow of the ice and they form the most striking physical features of the area. Between them lie low-lying plains often with a lake or marsh in the centre. The very hummocky relief makes the drainage of water very difficult especially as the soils are clayey. The drumlin exerts a powerful influence on the distribution of farmsteads. The house and farmyard often lie at the top of the drumlin in the driest but most windy site, but they can also be found lower down on one of the longer flanks where they are protected from the wind but where the land is less well drained. The hedgerows follow the contour of the drumlin with one along the long axis and others at right-angles to it down the flanks. Roads are difficult to make and must wind their way amidst the hills and hollows.

This kind of drumlin country (Fig. 42) occupies the whole area between Portadown, Loughgall and Richhill and forms the landscape of the fruit country. The orchards lie on the slopes of the drumlins so avoiding the frost pockets which often develop in the hollows. The Lough to the north reduces the amount of spring frost and so helps to avoid the destruction of apple blossom. The apple flowers later than the pear or plum which makes it less liable to be destroyed by frost (Fig. 43).

The soils are medium or rather heavy clay loams and are worked in farms of from 20 to 50 acres (8–20 ha). On most of these farms about one-third of the land will be given up to orchards, producing mostly Bramley's Seedling (a cooking apple) although dessert apples are being grown in larger quantities. Little cultivation is carried on – perhaps a few acres of potatoes or oats on each farm. Most of the land is used for pasture, silage and hay and herds of 8 to 10 Ayrshire or Friesian cows are kept for their milk. Pigs, too, are often important with 2–3 sows and 8–10 fatteners on each farm. Up to 200 poultry in deep litter are found on the farms almost everywhere.

Towards the north-east orchards become fewer, especially between Portadown and Lurgan and small fruit, notably strawberries (Fig. 44) increase in importance, often covering from 5 to 10 per cent of the farm area. This usage extends eastwards into the Lagan valley at Maze and Moira. Strawberries need to be marketed quickly and with Belfast, Lisburn, Lurgan and Portadown so near and connected by good road and rail transport, the area is well placed. Vegetables, rhubarb, raspberries and blackcurrants are also grown, the peaty soils along the fringes of the bogs being particularly favourable for them.

Although much of the fruit is sold fresh, preserving has become an important industry. Both Portadown and Richhill are centres for canning and jam-making (Fig. 45).

On the eastern fringe of the fruit country lies the largest town, Portadown. It lies astride the river Bann at a point where two ridges of glacial drift come close enough to the river to form a dry causeway across the low-lying wet lands of the Bann valley. High level bridges carry both road and railway across the river (Fig. 46). At this point the routes from Belfast via the Lagan valley, from Newry and Dublin to the

42. The drumlin country near Loughall, showing fruit, corn (oats) and grassland. Note the position of the orchard on the drumlin slope

43. The position of orchards on the drumlins

▒ Orchards   ↘ Cooling heavy air moves down into the hollows   ▭ Frosty areas by morning

26

south and from Armagh, Monaghan and Enniskillen to the south-west meet the route through Dungannon which fringes the southern shores of the Lough. Portadown has long been a major railway and road junction and now with the construction of the first motorway it lies at a vital point in relation to it. With its industries, which include linen, engineering, furniture making and several food processing plants, it is the most important town in central Ulster. Its population had reached 21 998 in 1971 and it is linked with Lurgan, some six miles (9.5 km) east, to form a large city named Craigavon.

Farm 1: A Typical Fruit Farm (Fig. 47)
This farm, which lies about 5 miles (8 km) west of Portadown near Annaghmore, typifies much of the fruit farm country of Co. Armagh. The farm is small, about 26 acres (10½ ha), although its size has been increased by renting an additional 20 acres (8 ha) which is 1½ miles (2½ km) away. It lies on a drumlin where it rises up out of the bogs to the south of Lough Neagh. It is a hilly and well-drained site but the soils are rather heavy clay except along the fringes of the bog.

The farm activities are varied. There is a dairy herd of 10–18 Friesian cows. All the calves produced are kept and reared, the heifers to join the milking herd and the bullocks fattened for beef. In all there will be as many as 40 cattle on the farm. Each cow averages 800 gallons (3636 litres) of milk per lactation. Milk is one of the major commodities sold.

Much land must be used to maintain the herd. The land is in a six-year ley rotation whilst hay is taken from the rented land. Associated with the animal husbandry are the orchard and other crops. The orchard – 3 acres (1.2 ha) of apples (Laxton Superb and Bramleys) – lies on the drumlin, faces southeast and is high enough to avoid the worst of the frosts. It produces 300–400 50 lb (22.7 kg) boxes of apples per acre and these are sold often for export to Britain. In addition, lettuce is grown outdoors whilst a glasshouse provides warmth for tomatoes. Along the edge of the

44. Strawberry picking at Richhill

45. Canning strawberries at Richhill

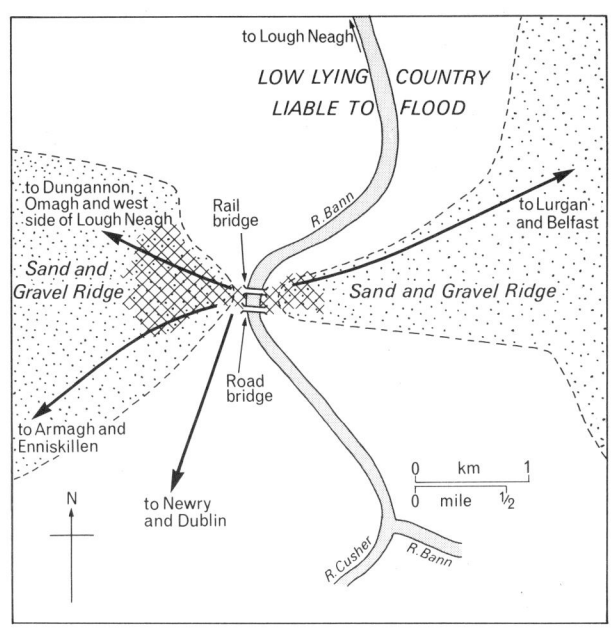
46. The site of Portadown

27

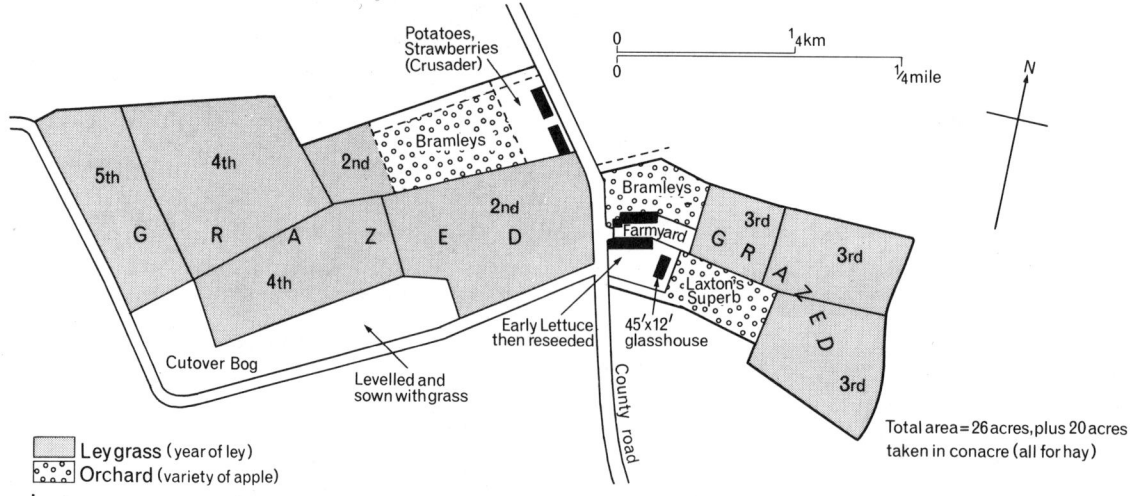

47. Farm 1: A fruit farm near Annaghmore

bog where the peat has been cleared, the soils suit early potatoes and strawberries of which about ¾ acre (0.3 ha) is grown. Nearness to Belfast and Portadown provides ready markets for these crops.

This is a well-equipped farm with a milking machine, tractor, hay-making and fruit-spraying equipment. The buildings have been renewed during the last ten years. It is owned by the farmer who does all the work with the occasional help of his brother.

Questions on the map of Lough Neagh (Fig. 37)

1. Measure (*a*) the length of Lough Neagh from Toome to Maghery, (*b*) the width from Ballyronan to Ardmore Point.

2. By using a piece of transparent graph paper work out the area of Lough Neagh.

3. Count the rivers flowing into Lough Neagh. How many rivers flow out? Does the difference between the two suggest any problems which may arise?

4. What is the name of the river which drains the Lough by way of Coleraine?

5. If the level of the surface of the water at Toome is 50 ft above sea-level what is the average gradient along this river from the Lough to the sea? Does this tell you anything about the rate of flow of the river?

6. Draw a section from Slieve Gallion (1737′) to Crew Hill (635′). What does this show about the relief of the area?

Questions on the L.U.S. map of the area south of Lough Neagh (Fig. 40)

1. The blacked areas show the orchards except near the town where they are housing estates. Omitting the town areas, make a tracing of the orchards. Describe their size and distribution over the area. Mark on your tracing Loughgall and Portadown. What other types of land use are found in this area?

2. What land use occurs between these fruitlands and the shores of Lough Neagh? Make a diagrammatic map of the north-west corner of the L.U.S. map to show (i) the bogs, (ii) the higher mounds with farms, (iii) the small enclosed areas of the 100 ft contour which show the drumlins. Is there any relationship between these three?

3. What is the effect of the valley of the river Bann on the distribution of orchards?

4 | CO. FERMANAGH AND THE SOUTH-WEST

The block transect (Fig. 48) drawn across Co. Fermanagh shows a part of Northern Ireland which is very different from much of the rest of the country. It is an area which drains by way of the river Erne and its lakes direct to the Atlantic Ocean in Sligo Bay. Its rainfall ranges from 40 to 50 inches (102–127 cm) a year in the lowlands and is much higher in the highlands. It is one of the wettest areas of Northern Ireland. The rain occurs throughout the year but with a maximum often in August and September. Farming is very difficult as the soils are leached by the heavy rainfall, the drainage is often poor due to the clay soils, and the harvest season for hay and corn is wet.

Furthermore its position far from the main centres of population and from the ports makes transport lengthy and costly and restricts the opportunities for trade. Market gardening, which could benefit from the mildness of the climate, is not possible without accessible markets.

The lands to the west of Lough Erne fall naturally into ridges and valleys of which the river Erne valley is the largest. This is flanked by the low Cullen Hills which are in turn divided from the much higher Belmore ridge by the Derrygonelly–Monea valley. Beyond the Belmore ridge the land falls quite rapidly to the beautiful valley of Loughs Macnean and the Arney river (Fig. 49) and then rises again to the high, flat-topped Cuilcagh Mountains on the border of the Irish Republic.

Rocks over the whole of this area are very old. Grits, shales and limestones are all found. They lie almost in horizontal beds, a fact which shows up in the flat-topped hills and the step-like character of many of their slopes. Erosion, both chemical and mechanical, has been responsible for carving out the major relief features (Fig. 50). Ice must have played a large part in this process but it has also been responsible for spreading drifts of 300–400 ft (91–122 m) in thickness over the lowlands. This boulder clay rises a hundred feet or more in the form of drumlins and falls between them into hollows occupied by ill-drained pastures and

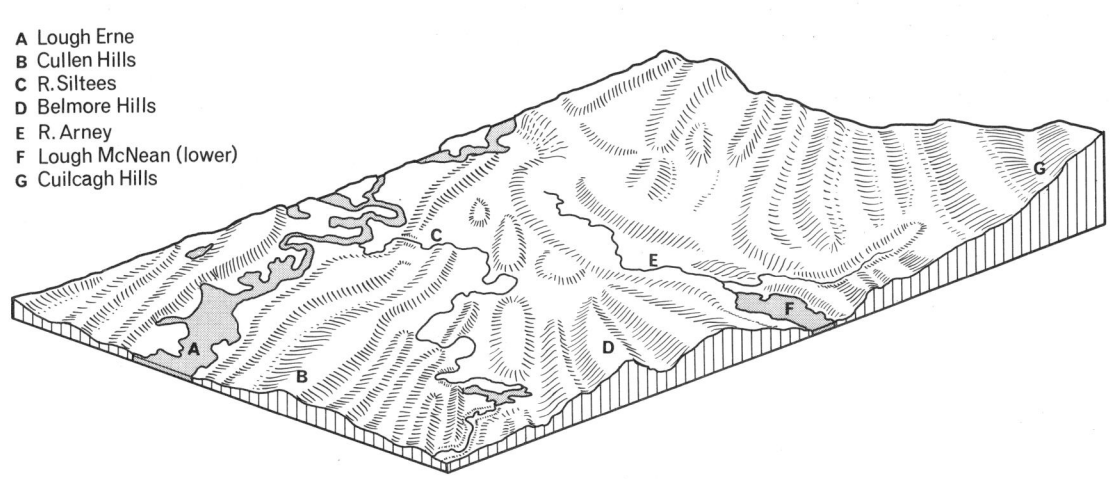

A Lough Erne
B Cullen Hills
C R. Siltees
D Belmore Hills
E R. Arney
F Lough McNean (lower)
G Cuilcagh Hills

48. Block transect of Co. Fermanagh

49. A view across Lough Macnean, with the flat top of the mountains visible beyond

peat bogs. Often the drumlins stand up in the lakes as elongated islands (Fig. 51). Much of the beauty of Lough Erne derives from the many islands clothed with trees which are scattered in it. Everywhere the drumlins lie in rows, parallel to the flow of the ice which made them, and with their blunt and tapering ends form a major feature of the lowland landscape. Such lakeside beauty attracts many tourists and tourism as an industry is being encouraged.

Upon the higher mountains the soils are thin and poor, and grazing is the only farm usage although increasing areas are being forested with Sitka spruce and other conifers. Often the mountain farms are large to secure enough pasturage to maintain flocks of sheep and herds of cattle. Generally the farms in the lower country are small, being less than 30 acres (12 ha) and often under 20 (8 ha). On these small farms there is usually an acre or two of crops – oats or potatoes – whilst the rest of the land is used for grazing. Small dairy herds supply milk to the Whitewell and other creameries whilst store bullocks add to the animal population. These are sold to be fattened upon better pastures elsewhere in Ireland or Britain. Poultry and pigs, fed on purchased foodstuffs, are found on most of the farms; they need little space. This is a hard land to farm, yields are low and the living which it provides is often meagre. Its heavy, often waterlogged soils, the high water table and the peats make farming arduous and uncertain.

The lowland between the Belmore Hills and the Cullen Hills is drained towards Lough Erne at Enniskillen by the Siltees river. It is a land of drumlins fashioned in very sticky blue boulder clay. There is little seepage of water and the run-off is slow. Lakes and peat bogs occupy the lowest parts. Pastures are poor and infested with rush (Fig. 52). The farms are very small (15–20 acres, 6½–8 ha) and these are broken down into a large number of very small fields. A few, often only two or three, cows are kept and the calves are sold off when they are young. Most of the farmers rely on pigs and poultry in deep litter – the two enterprises which can be carried on in a small area and to a large extent under cover. Little land is fit for cultivation and often the half-acre or so which is tilled is dug by spade. These small cultivated plots are located around the edges of the peat bogs where cultivation is easier than on the clay and where the soils are often more fertile.

The Cullen Hills (600–700′, 182–213 m) are better drained and much drier. Limestones crop out on the surface and the clays are less common. Larger farms up to 60 acres (24 ha)

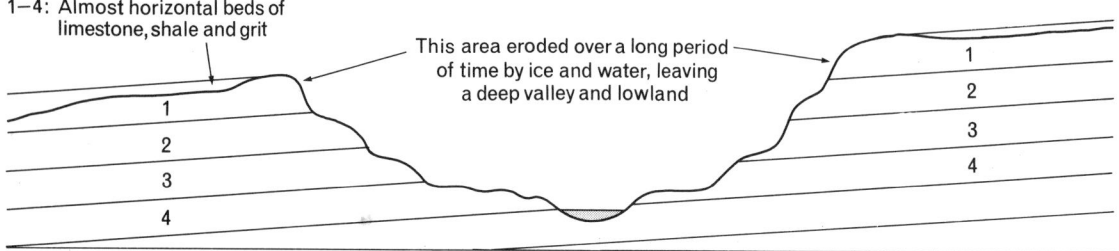

50. Formation of the major relief features of Co. Fermanagh

provide better working conditions. More land is tilled for oats and potatoes whilst rotation grasses help to improve the pasture. Dairy farming is important and herds of 20 cows or more are usual. Sheep, too, are increasing in numbers. Derrygonnelly forms a small centre in the midst of this region.

Beyond the Cullen Hills stretches the large lowland basin occupied by the river Erne and its two loughs. It lies mainly on Old Red Sandstone rocks, is bounded on the west by the steep edge of the Carboniferous Limestone series, and to the north by a rugged schist plateau. Thus Lower Lough Erne lies in a rock basin which has been fashioned by ice and which is deep enough to fall below sea-level. This lake area has been very liable to flooding and the natural drainage has been slow and often impeded. Recently drainage works have reduced the flood risk and made possible the generation of electricity on the Falls of Erne near Ballyshannon, just within the Irish Republic. Belleek, which is a bridging point at the lower end of the Lough, is noted for high quality china. The development of electric power in this area is important as it provides a source of power in an area short of fuel and a long distance from the coast. The establishment of nylon clothing and stocking making at Enniskillen is an example of how supplies of power can help in the establishment of industry.

In the Erne valley, drainage and soil type are the important factors in farming. Around the lakes there are many waterlogged peaty hollows between the drumlins and these add to the difficulties of the farmer. On the drumlin-covered lowland towards Irvinestown in the east the boulder clays are very sticky and the soils are heavy clay loams. Drainage is not good and very little tillage is possible. A few acres of oats and vegetables are the only crops. The farms are small (20–25 acres, 8–10 ha) and only small herds of dairy cows are possible, the milk going to the Irvinestown centre. Further south-east towards Ballinamallard the soils become lighter. Farms are still often small but their size varies and a few may be as large as 300 acres (120 ha). Up to 20 per cent of their

51. Lough Erne, showing the islands, which are partially drowned drumlins

area may be cultivated for oats or potatoes whilst much of the rest is in grassland, often improved by re-seeding and fertilisation. Silage-making has also become important – a valuable change from hay-making (Fig. 53) in such a wet area. Also by adopting stall feeding in winter more cattle can be maintained in good condition throughout the year. Dairying has grown in importance with larger herds, and in some cases pedigree stock is kept. Most farmers have a few sows and rear pigs whilst many keep from 150 to 200 hens in deep litter. Added to these activities are sheep fattening and beef production. This area is much

52. Lough Erne, showing the poor pastures of the lowest parts, infested with rush

53. Hay-making in the Erne valley: the whole family takes part

54. A typical small farm in Co. Fermanagh

wealthier and more prosperous than those to the west of the lake.

In the south-western part of Northern Ireland there is a very close relationship between the prosperity of farming and the relief, drainage and type of soil. Light soils, especially on well-drained drumlin slopes or glacial outwash sands and gravels, tend to be more valuable. With the laying of field drains to help in the removal of the excessive moisture, the area of useful farm land is being extended.

The farmsteads (Fig. 54), like those in all parts of Northern Ireland, are scattered singly about the countryside. Many of them have become derelict because of migration from the land and the coalescence of very small holdings into larger and more economic units. The study of the farm which follows is typical of many of the more prosperous farms which are found in this part of Northern Ireland.

Farm 2: A farm (40 acres 16.2 ha) on the shores of Lough Erne (Fig. 55)

The farm is owned by two brothers who do all the work between them. They rent a further 9 acres (3.6 ha) about 10 miles (16 km) away. The farm itself lies about ½ mile (0.8 km) from the main road along a loaning (farm lane) which has recently been concreted to make access to the farm easier and cleaner. The soil is heavy clay. Drainage of the land would be very hard in any case and it is made more difficult by the hummocky relief caused by the drumlins.

With such difficult land little cultivation is carried on. Except for a small garden and one field the farm is entirely in permanent grass. The grass is improved by the use of fertilisers and weed killers in spring.

Pig rearing forms the major activity. Up to 250 pigs are bought in when they are 8–12 weeks old and kept for 12 weeks to reach bacon weight. This scheme of fattening is undertaken four times in each year. All the food for the pigs is purchased and includes meal as well as skimmed milk from the local creamery at Derrygonnelly. There are also 50 hens and 100 broilers reared indoors and fed on purchased food.

There is a herd of 25 cows (Friesian and crossbred) whose milk is fed to the calves. The calves are not fully fattened but are kept for

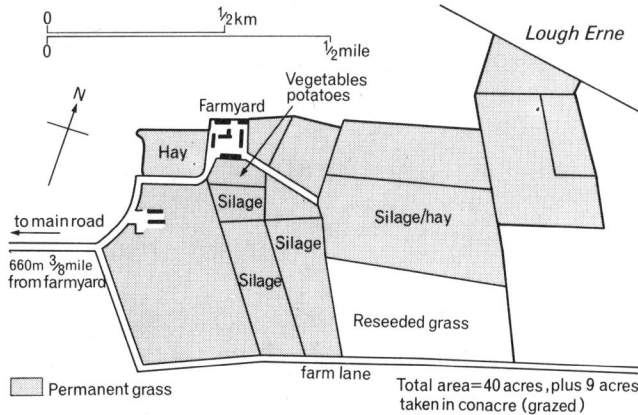

55. **Farm 2: A farm on the shores of Lough Erne**

about 18 months and then sold to be finished for market elsewhere. 170 tons (172.7 metric tons) of silage and 400 bales of hay are made to provide winter feed for the cattle. They are grazed in summer on the rented land.

The farmstead has been much improved from older buildings and is now mainly piggeries and broiler houses.

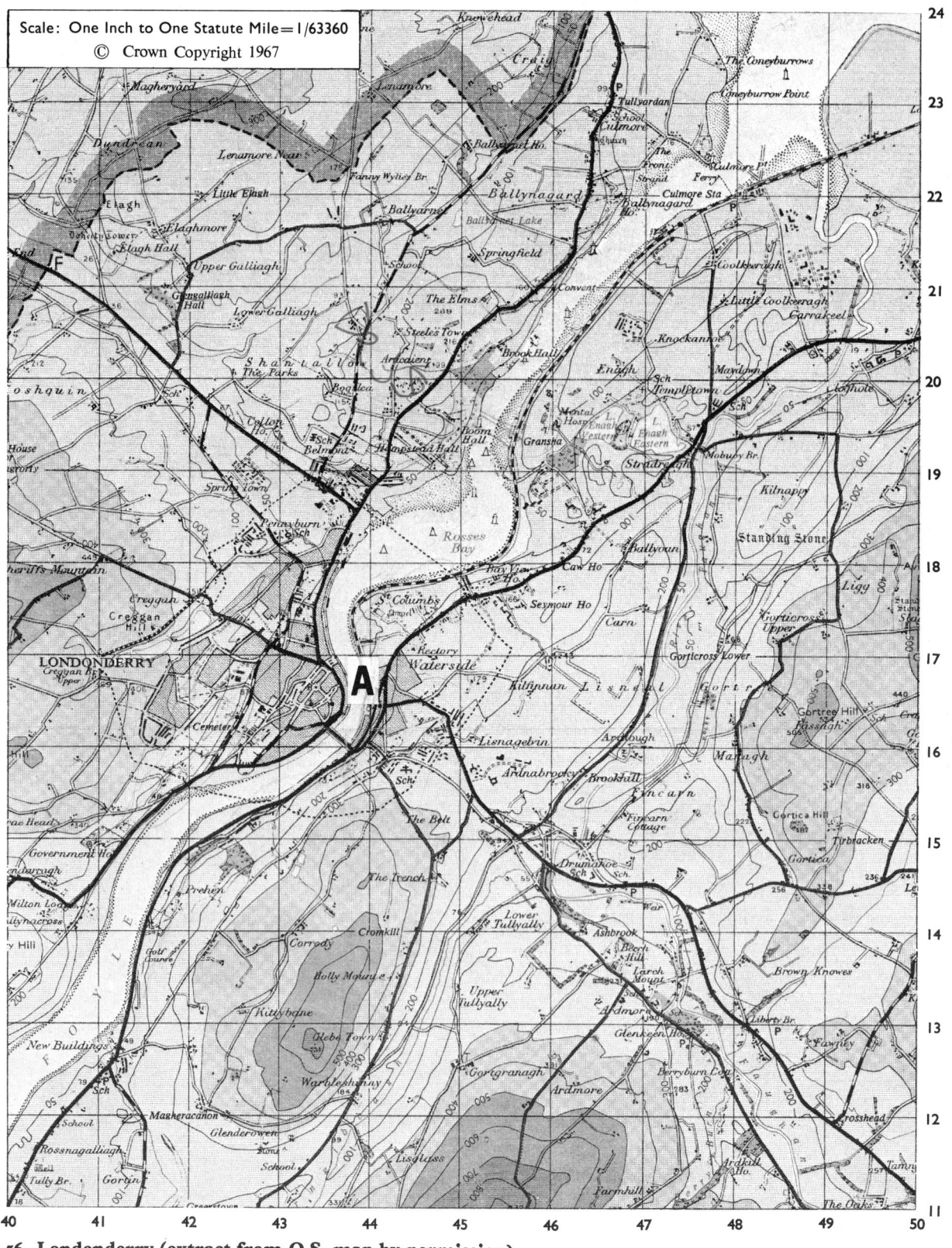

56. Londonderry (extract from O.S. map by permission)

5 LONDONDERRY

Londonderry (Fig. 56), the largest town in the north-west of Northern Ireland, is situated on the river Foyle about 24 miles (38 km) from the sea. It is the chief port and the focal centre for those parts of the north of Ireland west of the Sperrin Mountains and the hills of north Derry. To the southward its hinterland stretches beyond the Foyle valley to Enniskillen and the river Erne valley. To the west lies Co. Donegal in the Irish Republic. It does some trade with Co. Donegal but the presence of the Border nearby reduces it considerably.

Derry (Fig. 57) lies on the west bank of the river Foyle and it is surrounded on three sides by a large meander. On the landward side to the west a low-lying boggy valley separates it from the rest of the country. This low-lying valley was occupied by an abandoned channel of the river Foyle. Opposite the city on the east bank a ridge comes close to the river at a point where the river narrows before spreading out into the wide Rosses Bay below the city. It is thus a natural crossing point which is now the site of the only bridge below Strabane – the Craigavon bridge.

People have lived on this site since about A.D. 545 whilst a monastic settlement existed there in the tenth century. However, the city,

57. Aerial photograph taken above point A on the map (Fig. 56) and looking approximately west-south-west

like so many north Irish towns, came into existence first as a military outpost and then as an English Plantation town in the early years of the seventeenth century. It has a striking site. Besides being almost surrounded by the river Foyle, its heart, the Diamond, lies on the top of a hill. Thus it grew on a dry, defensible site which was further strengthened by the building of the massive wall which still remains intact today (Fig. 58).

The old city, within the wall, provides the commercial centre of a much larger modern city which has spread in every direction beyond the wall and has crossed the river to Waterside on the east bank.

From the Diamond (Fig. 59) the main streets run down the sides of the hill towards the old gates in the wall. The largest and most expensive shops centre around the Diamond but shops extend down Ferryquay Street, Bishops Street and Butcher Street, whilst the steep Shipquay Street is lined by banks and offices. Also within the old walls are St Columbs Cathedral, the Court House and the County Offices. The Guildhall, the centre of the city administration, was built in 1912 just outside Shipquay Gate, between it and the quay (Fig. 58). The Post Office and Customs House are nearby. Expansion beyond the walls is a marked feature of the modern city, with many institutions including The Institute of Continuing Education of the new University of Ulster at Magee, the Museum and the Althagelvin Hospital all outside the walls together with much of the industry.

Londonderry is a port. The riverside wharves lie where the deepest channel of the river Foyle comes close to the west bank. The river has never been easy to navigate, its bed tending to silt up whilst it is narrowed at Culmore Point by a large sandspit. Dredging is necessary to keep the channel clear and to deepen it to take larger ships. The connection with the sea goes back into the eighteenth and

58. Londonderry: the Wall, Shipquay Gate and the Guildhall

59. The Diamond in Londonderry. Diamond is a name given to the central square in several towns of N. Ireland

SHEET 3 MAP A

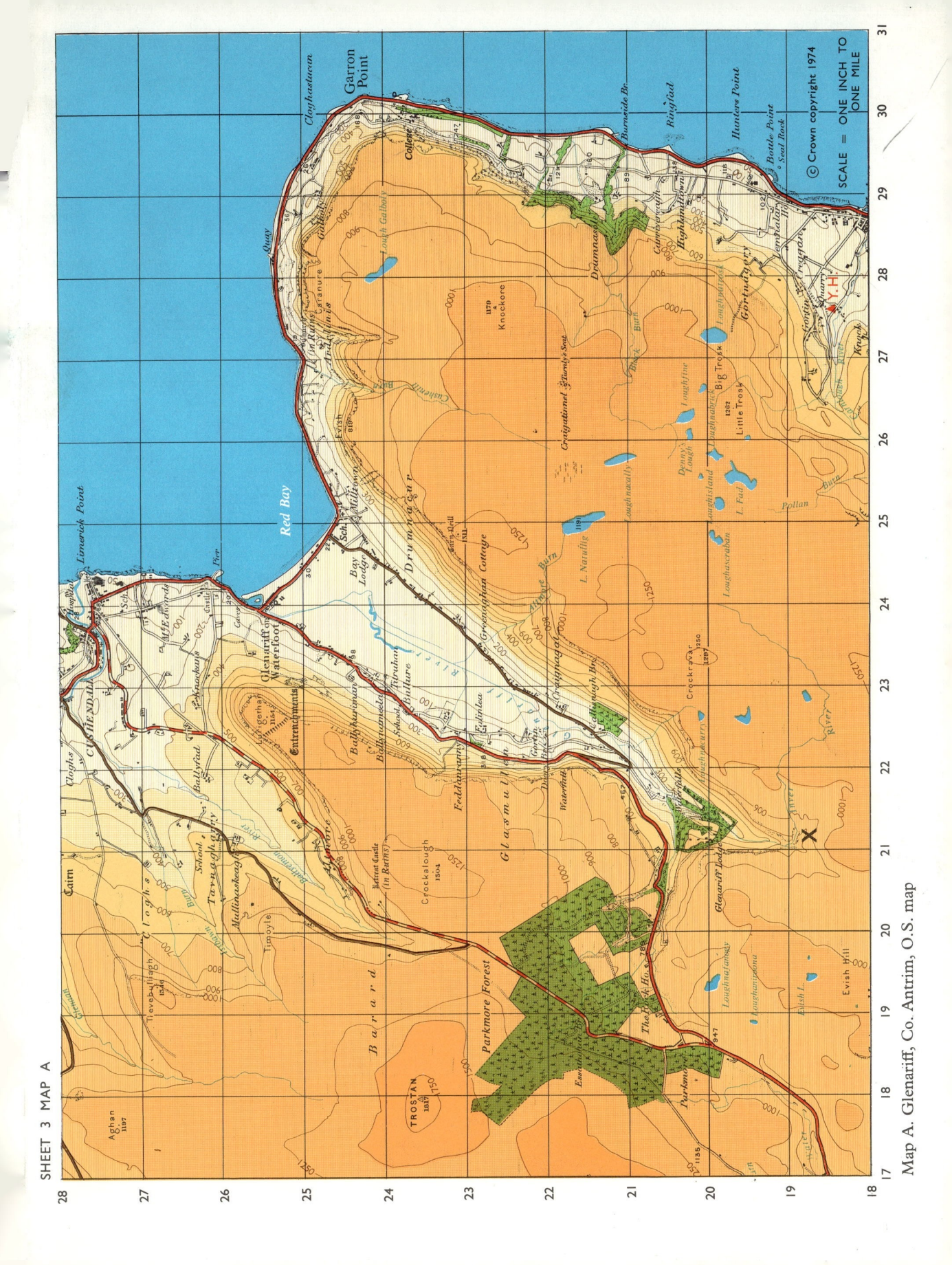

Map A. Glenariff, Co. Antrim, O.S. map

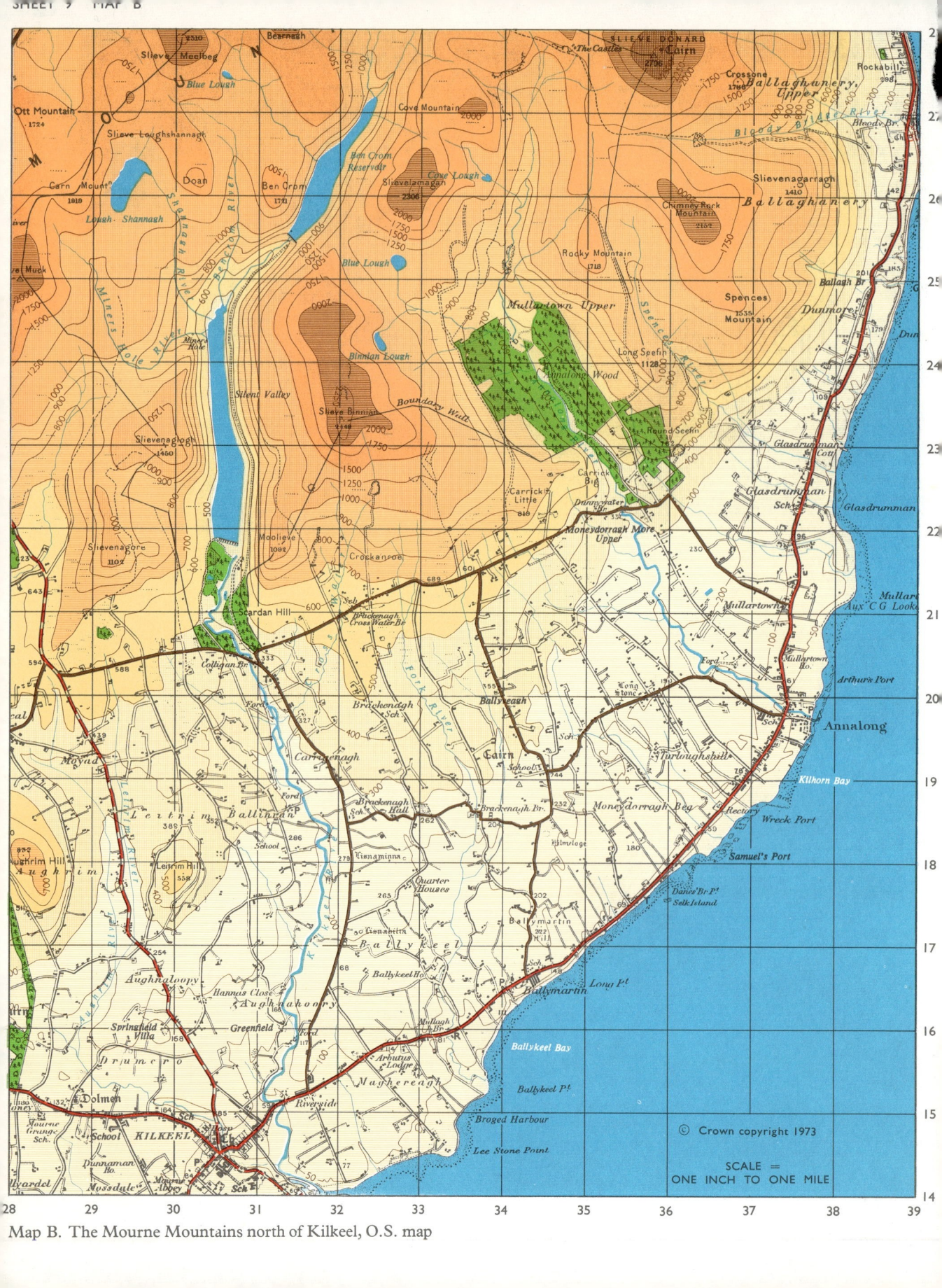

Map B. The Mourne Mountains north of Kilkeel, O.S. map

SHEET 3 MAP C

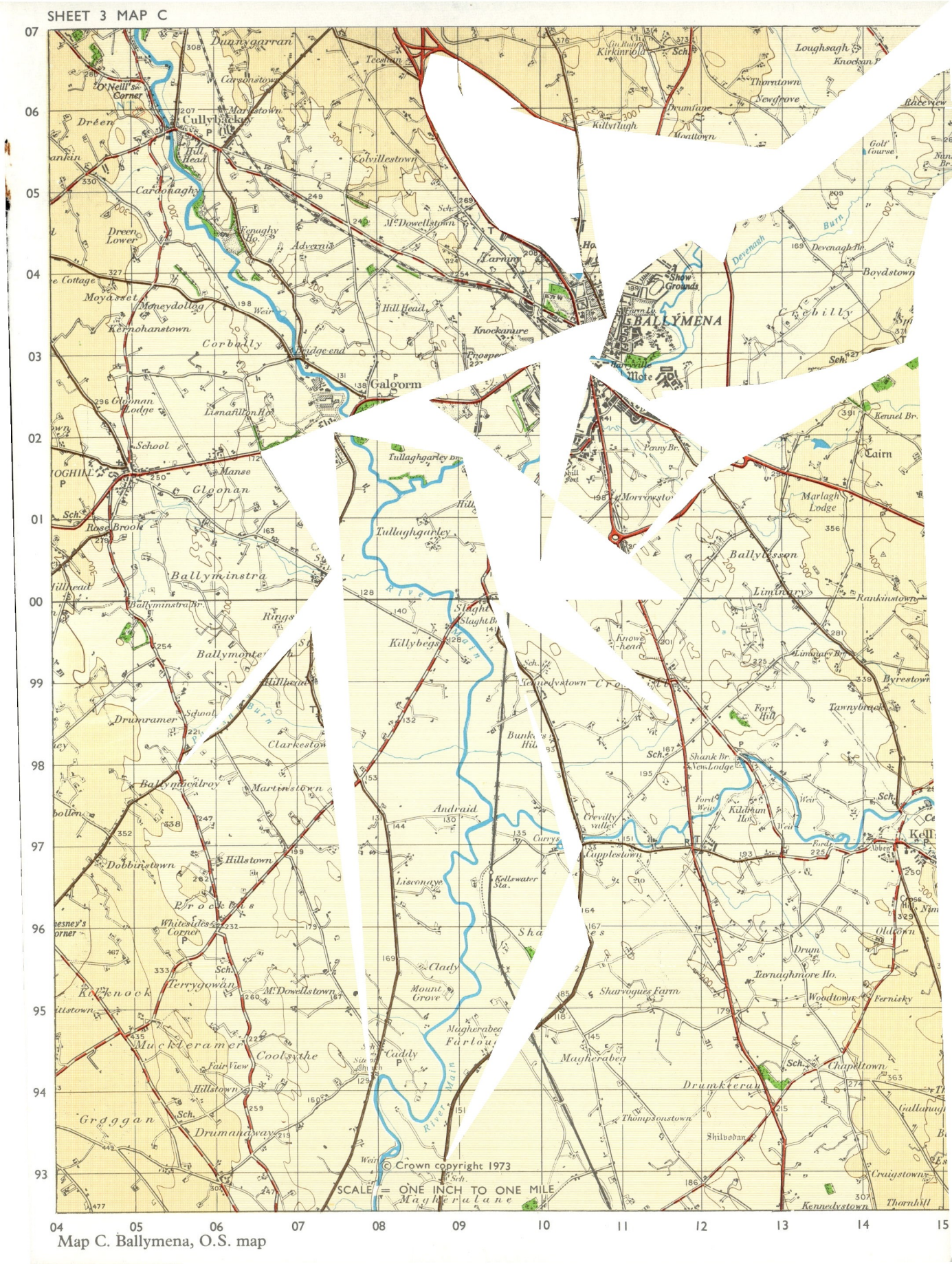

Map C. Ballymena, O.S. map

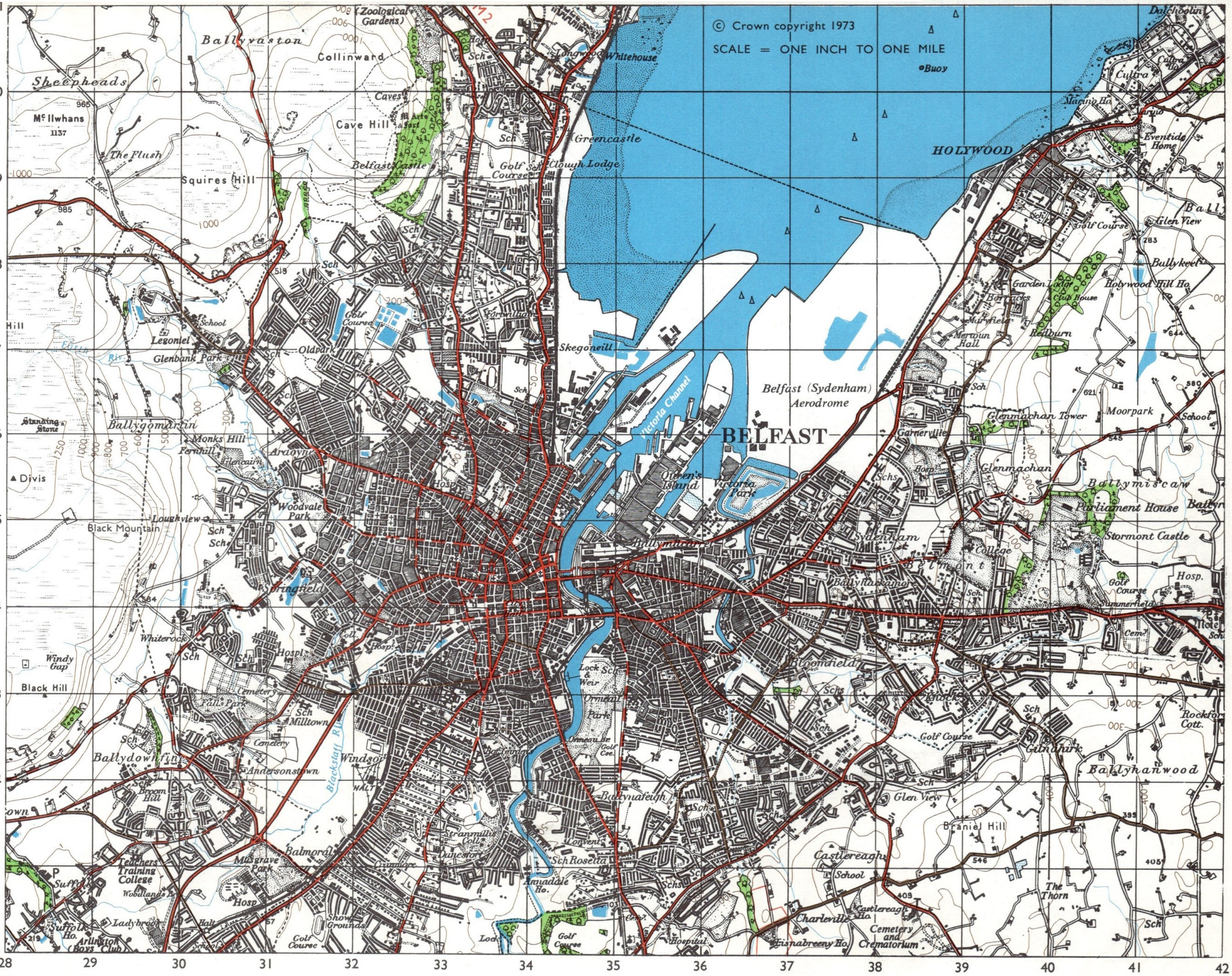

Map D. Belfast O.S. map

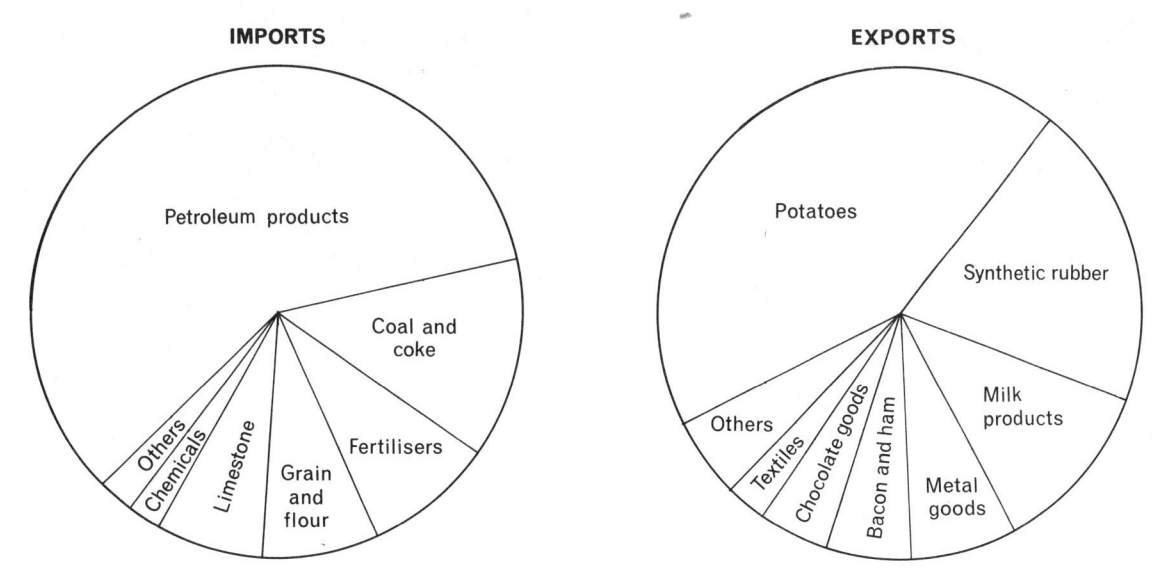

60. Trade of the port of Londonderry (by tonnage, percentage of total)

nineteenth centuries when the city had extensive trade with America and Europe as well as with Glasgow and Liverpool. Since that period the trade has fluctuated in amount and its character has changed. Recently trade has developed with the new industries. It is an important port for petroleum products used in the surrounding area and especially at the new power station at Coolkeeragh. Large new factories manufacturing synthetic materials and oxygen have increased the imports of raw materials, especially limestone and chemicals. At the same time it remains a port for coal and coke from South Wales, for fertilisers from Middlesbrough and timber from Scandinavia.

Londonderry's exports (Fig. 60) have not grown at the same rate as its imports. Livestock exports have declined in the last ten years but potatoes for other countries, especially along the Mediterranean, have reached 43 per cent of all exports. Synthetic products are exported whilst pit-props from the forests on the Derry Hills now replace the ballast in the empty coal boats going back to South Wales.

Cross-channel cargo boats ply to Glasgow and other ports throughout the year.

From an industrial point of view Londonderry is perhaps best known for its shirtmaking and clothing industry (Fig. 61). Factories, often owned by firms from England, are located in many parts of the city, several adjoining the quayside warehouses. Waterside also shares in this industry. Over half the working population, mainly women, is employed in this industry. Textiles, including linen, have been made in the city for many years and now employ about 23 per cent of the workers. Food, drinks and tobacco industries and the building and

61. Employment in Londonderry (percentage of total registered workers)

other construction industries have 9 per cent each. The newer industries – artificial fibres, oxygen and rubber – account for another 10 per cent. Shipbuilding, for a long time an important industry, has ceased.

There is not enough industry in the city to provide employment for all its people, and many, especially men, are unemployed. In 1973 the average unemployment for men and women was 13.9%; 19.06 for men and 6.4 for women. Further industry is needed, especially to provide employment for men. Much of the present industry, notably shirtmaking, provides little male employment (e.g. in one shirt factory only 10% of the labour force are men).

In the twenty years (1951–71) the population has grown from 50 092 to 52 205, with a peak of 55 694 in 1966, which has led to a need for more houses. Nearly 4000 have been built in the last twenty years, many in housing estates but also a number of larger houses amongst the pleasant undulating countryside on the fringes of the city. Many more will be needed not only to house the growing population but also to replace the many decaying houses in the older parts of the city. This work has already begun and large blocks of modern flats may now be seen where once were narrow streets of cramped terrace houses.

62. Aerial photograph of Central Ballymena

6 BALLYMENA

Ballymena (Colour Map C and Fig. 62) lies in the centre of Co. Antrim, 28 miles (45 km) north-north-east of Belfast on the main route to the north coast and Londonderry. It is sited at a crossing point of the river Braid (Fig. 63) where the 200 ft (61 m) contour comes close to the banks of the river. At first this point was occupied by a ford and later by a bridge, the higher ground making it easier to approach the river across a low-lying marshy valley.

The importance of this crossing point was evident very early in the settlement of north-east Ireland. The light sandy soil of the Braid valley to the east attracted man and the nine great megalithic monuments which occur in the valley testify to settlement as early as the Bronze Age. In the eighth century A.D. the area became famous because St Patrick is said to have lived near Sleamish Mountain whilst the crossing point was used by a road from Tara – the then capital of Ireland – to Dunseverick on the north coast.

Although there are these early evidences of people living in the area around Ballymena, the town itself began to develop in the seventeenth century at the time when Plantations of English and Scottish people were settling in Ireland. Ballymena seems to owe its origin to Scottish settlers, especially the Adair family. By the middle of the seventeenth century a small

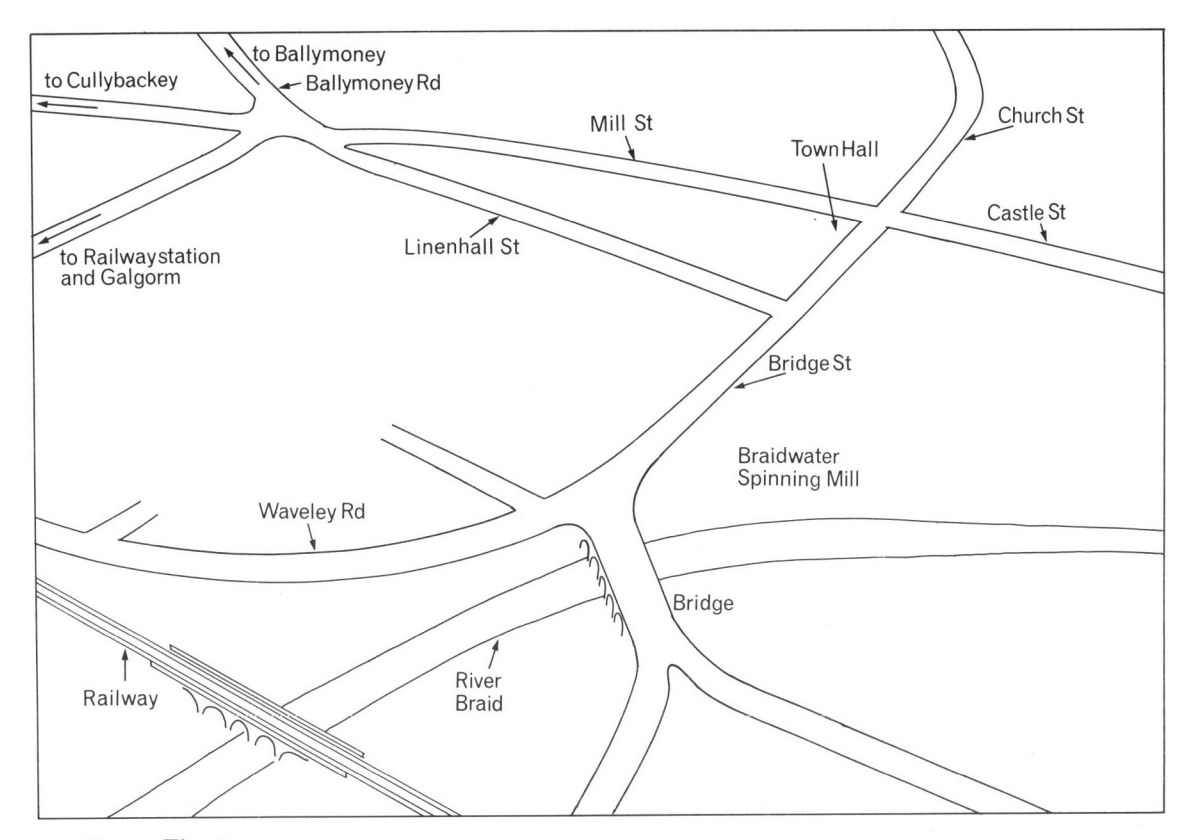

63. Key to Fig. 62

market had been established and later in the same century a market house was built on the site of the present Town Hall (Fig. 64) at the corner of Mill Street. By the end of the century over a hundred houses clustered round it whilst the two main streets crossed here – Mill Street/Castle Street leading towards the Anglo-Norman Castle and Church Street/Bridge Street leading to the river crossing. The town then grew away from the river on the higher ground in the direction of Galgorm.

At the beginning of the eighteenth century the first textile mill started in Ballymena. A weir was built above the town on the Braid and four bleaching mills were built in the town. By 1830 a beetling mill had been built and this was followed later in the nineteenth century by spinning and weaving mills (Fig. 62). Local flax was the chief raw material used and the linen industry developed from a domestic craft in the houses to a factory industry by the beginning of the twentieth century. With it the population increased from 1000 in 1800 to 10 000 (Fig. 65).

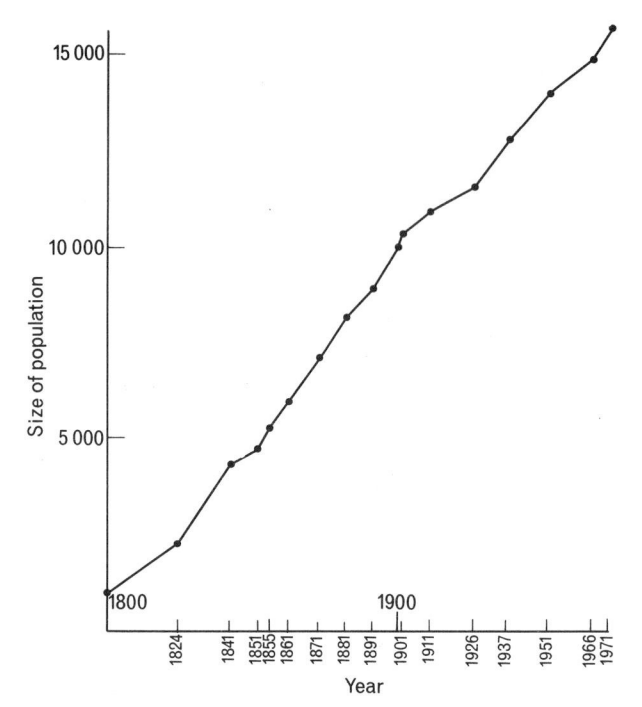

64. Ballymena: the Town Hall, at the corner of Mill Street

65. The growth of population in Ballymena, 1800-1971

The central position of Ballymena in Co. Antrim caused the market to expand as communications improved and the farms grew more efficient. The nineteenth century was marked by sales of potatoes, oats, flax, pigs and poultry, dairy produce, vegetables and linen. Street markets were usual at this time, different parts of the town specialising in one commodity (e.g. flax on Fair Hill, corn in Smithfield Square). By 1833 it was reputed to have the largest inland market in the country. Street widening was undertaken to help accommodate the traders, emphasising a problem which still persists. Horses and carts have now been replaced by cars which pack the streets (Fig. 66).

Marketing still remains very important and the town serves a large area around as well as the town itself. Produce and stock markets are still held on Fair Hill on three days a week. The many shops, grocers and provision merchants, hardware merchants, provender suppliers and agencies for farm implements all testify to its vital place in the farming industry of the area. The town is also a collecting centre for the Ministry of Agriculture's marketing schemes, whilst near the river are the large grounds of the Agricultural Show.

The combination of marketing, trading and industry forms the core of life in Ballymena. It continues to grow (population in 1971 – 16 503), expand in area and strengthen its influence on the surrounding countryside. The town has a major hospital, secondary schools, a large technical school, and has attracted several large new industries; it is the main bus and rail centre in Co. Antrim and publishes the chief local newspaper. It has now become the county town.

In plan Ballymena may be divided into four zones (Fig. 67) according to the chief use made of them. These are (1) the shopping and commercial zone, (2) the older residential zone, (3) the modern residential zone, and (4) the industrial zone.

(1) The Shopping and Commercial Zone centres around the Town Hall (Fig. 64) and spreads chiefly into Bridge Street, Mill Street and Church Street. The town is a good shopping centre for most of the necessities of life and also for the many needs of the farmers. Some small industries exist around the fringes of the shopping area and include saw mills, bakeries and metal works.

The streets are generally too narrow for the volume of traffic and one-way systems are used whilst there is a large car park near the Demesne. Nevertheless, the streets remain crowded with cars, vans and lorries (Fig. 66).

(2) Beyond the shopping area lies the older housing districts, mostly built in the nineteenth and early twentieth centuries and usually consisting of terrace houses in red brick (Fig. 68). The oldest cottages in Fair Hill and Alexander Street are single-storeyed with half-doors (Fig. 69), built of local stone and whitewashed on the outside. Slate has now replaced the original thatched roofs.

(3) Stretching from these central areas are the

66. Ballymena: Church Street, showing central shopping area and traffic congestion

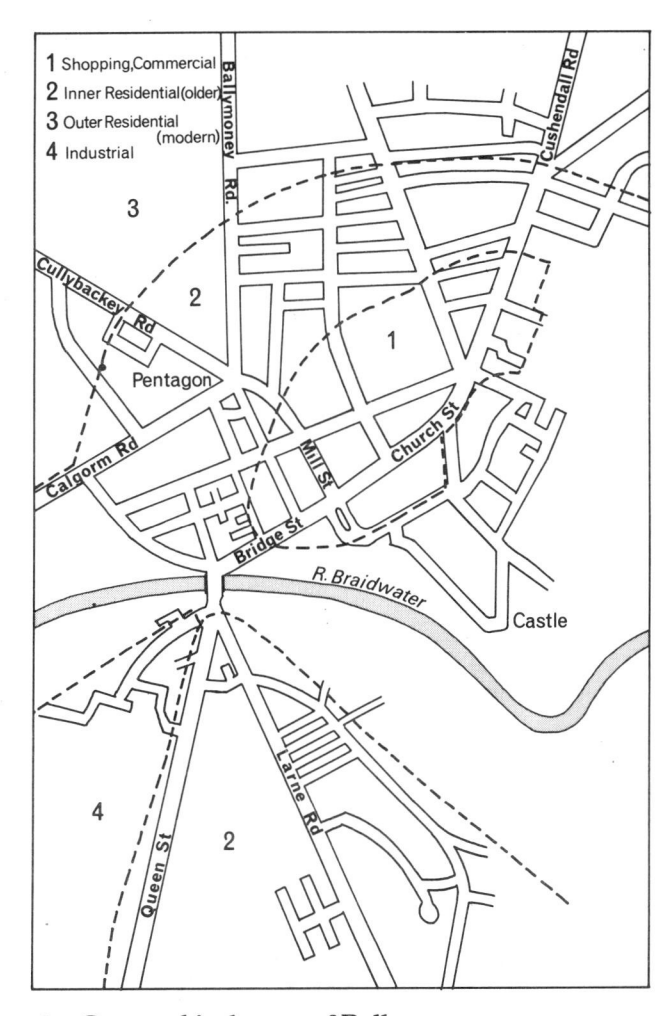

67. Geographical zones of Ballymena

68. Older housing in Zone 2

69. Oldest housing found in Zone 2

70. Post-war housing in Zone 3

newer houses, areas which consist of detached villas in their own grounds or smaller villas detached or semi-detached and mostly built between 1930 and 1940. These line the roads leading from Ballymena, often for as much as a mile from the town centre. New post-war housing estates have grown up in these same areas (Fig. 70).

(4) Industry has developed since the nineteenth century. Textiles, especially linen but also wool, cotton and man-made fibres, and food processing, are the two chief groups. There are also boot and shoe, shirtmaking and tobacco factories whilst several branches of engineering are locally important. Industry tends to keep close to the river and forms an industrial district in Harryville on the south bank. Just across the river and overlooking the bridge is the large Braidwater Mill. Industrial expansion is taking place in the Braidwater valley where a large tyre factory has been established, whilst beyond Galgorm at Gracehill are tobacco factories.

Fig. 71 shows the centres of convergence of main roads on Ballymena. It has a strong nodal position in central Antrim and forms a major transport centre for both passenger and freight traffic. As such it is the transport and supply centre of the large area stretching from the east coast to the river Bann, with a population of 65 000 to 70 000 people. A new motorway now by-passes the town.

The area, including the towns of Ballymena and Antrim, has been designated a growth area to be developed as a major city of Northern Ireland. Already new industry in the form of a large artificial fibre factory is beginning to develop on land between the two towns.

71. Ballymena, major road junctions

Questions on Colour Map C

1. Make a tracing from the map to show:
   (a) (i) The chief rivers with their names,
       (ii) The 200 ft contour including any small isolated hills over this height,
       (iii) The bridge over the Braidwater.
   (b) With the aid of your tracing state briefly the facts which the map shows about the position of Ballymena.

2. Draw a sketch-map to show that Ballymena is an important route centre.

3. Ballymena means 'the settlement in the bog'. Why is this an appropriate name for a town situated here? Shade those areas which are less than 200 ft above sea-level.

4. Farms are usually between 200 ft and 400 ft above sea-level with a number between 400 ft and 600 ft. Make a map to show whether these statements are true or false.

43

7 | BELFAST

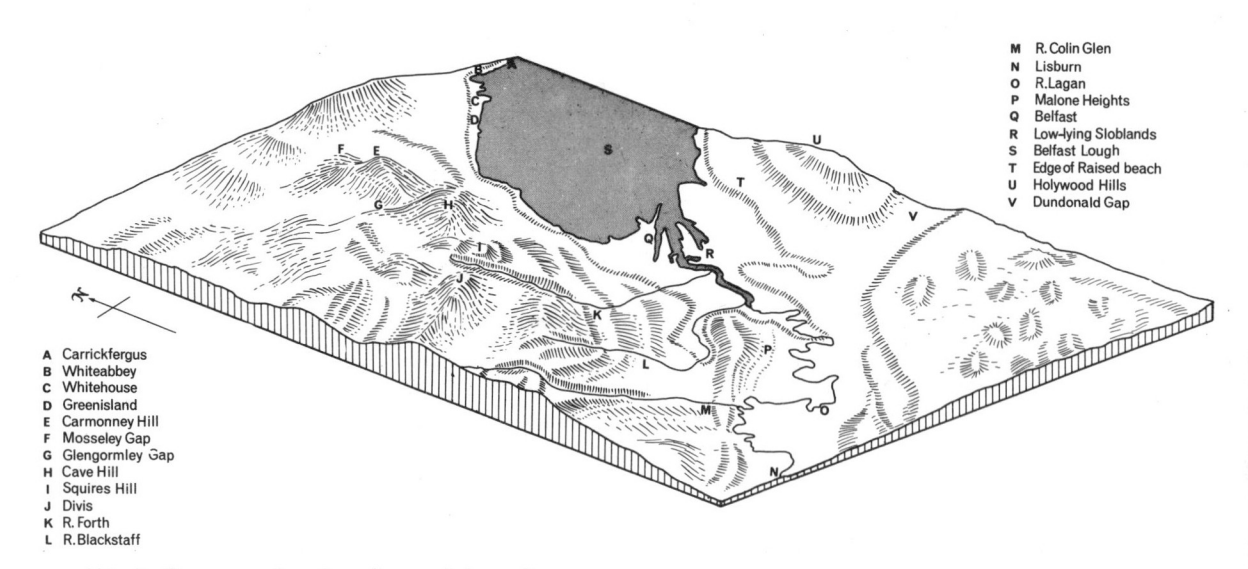

M R. Colin Glen
N Lisburn
O R. Lagan
P Malone Heights
Q Belfast
R Low-lying Sloblands
S Belfast Lough
T Edge of Raised beach
U Holywood Hills
V Dundonald Gap

A Carrickfergus
B Whiteabbey
C Whitehouse
D Greenisland
E Carmonney Hill
F Mosseley Gap
G Glengormley Gap
H Cave Hill
I Squires Hill
J Divis
K R. Forth
L R. Blackstaff

72. Block diagram showing the position of Belfast

Belfast has a very distinctive setting (Colour Map D), one which has much natural charm although industrial smog and bad planning have partly spoiled it. To the west and north within the city boundary lies the scarp face of the Antrim Plateau, rising in Cave Hill to 1112 feet (339 m). The city reaches the foot of this scarp and ascends wherever a gap, as at Glengormley, makes it possible to pass through it. To the south and east are the much lower, more rounded Holywood Hills which it also approaches. Between these two areas of hill country, some four to six miles (6–10 km) apart, is the great glaciated rift valley occupied to the north-east by Belfast Lough and to the south-west by the river Lagan. It is where these two meet that Belfast is situated (Fig. 72).

Since the end of the Great Ice Age the land has risen relatively to the sea and surrounding the whole centre of the city is the old sea-beach (i.e. a raised beach), some 20–25 ft (6–7½ m) above the present sea-level (Fig. 73). This beach is used by the roads entering the city

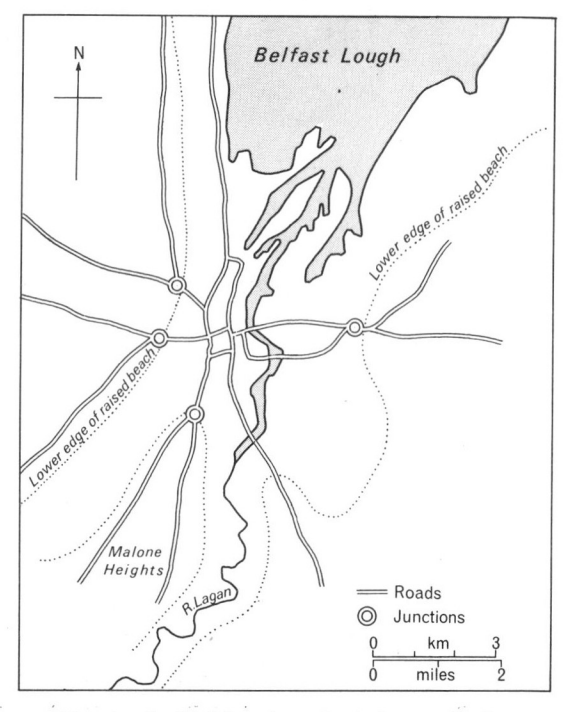

73. Routes in Belfast in relation to relief

44

from all directions and they cluster at its lower edge into road junctions (e.g. Bradbury Place), from which a few through roads cross the low-lying central area to reach and cross the river Lagan (Fig. 73).

The centre of Belfast lies on marine and river muds which have been and still are being deposited at the head of Belfast Lough. The central area is almost level and since the eighteenth century has been divided into rectangular blocks of buildings which are separated by wide and straight streets (Fig. 75). Drainage works have prevented frequent flooding. This flat mud area, locally called the Sloblands, has had two important effects on the growth of the city:

(i) It has been easy to straighten the lower part of the meandering river Lagan and to excavate the sea-basins and channels needed for the port and the shipbuilding industry. The excavated mud has provided sites for factories near the port.

(ii) All large buildings have been carefully constructed on piles, formerly of wood as in the case of the City Hall and now of steel and concrete. Most of the large buildings of the centre of the city float on rafts set in the mud and supported through the piles on the rock beneath it.

Belfast is essentially a city built of brick, often locally made from the Keuper marls, but within it are many contrasts and different districts contribute in various ways to the whole (Fig. 74). Six such districts stand out:

(1) Donegal Place, Donegal Square, Royal Avenue and the adjoining streets form the city centre with administrative buildings such as the City Hall, banking and insurance offices and the major shops (Fig. 75).

(2) The Western Areas which have many factories especially for linen (Fig. 76) and extensive working-class housing. Most of the factories originally owed their position to the several fast-flowing streams which descend from the South Antrim Hills. The water was used for power and for cleaning and processing the materials for the linen industry.

(3a) The Port Industrial Area lies along the banks of the river Lagan near to the docks, and

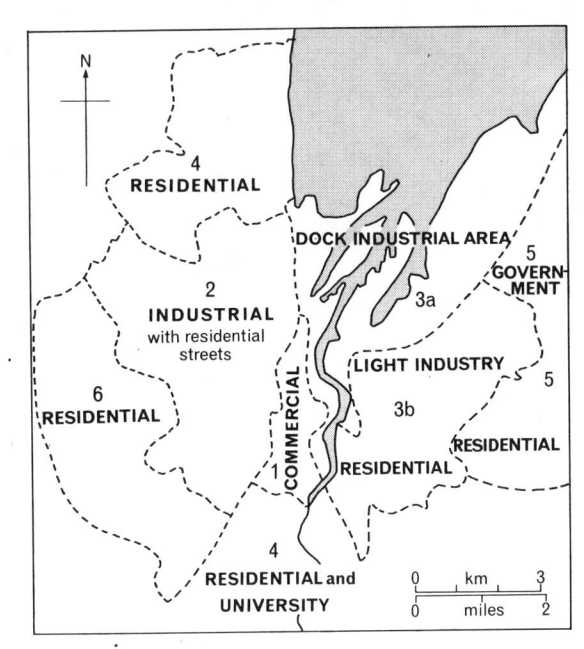

74. Geographical zones of Belfast

includes industries such as gas, electricity, shipbuilding, flour milling, and rope making, which need imported and heavy raw materials (Fig. 77). There are also extensive areas of working-class houses on both sides of the river.

(b) An area of light industry extends south-east from the dock area.

(4) The Residential Areas on the rising slopes of the Malone Ridge and on the Antrim Road below Cave Hill. Both areas contain the larger houses of the professional and business people and the former includes Queen's University and Stranmillis College of Education.

(5) The Government Building at Stormont forms the centre of another distinctive area which features many government offices as well as the extensive suburbs of Belmont, Knock, etc. Many civil servants live in this zone.

(6) This is a large area of suburban development which stretches south-west up the Lagan valley. It includes the middle-class 'Parks' of the nineteenth century and more recent pre-war and post-war housing which stretches beyond the city boundary at Balmoral to include Finaghy and Dunmurry (Fig. 78).

45

75. **Aerial view of Central Belfast, showing wide streets in a rectangular pattern**

Key
1 City Hall
2a Donegall Place
2b High Street
2c Royal Avenue
3 Technical College
4 Royal Belfast Academical Institute
5 Great Victoria Street Station
6 Assembly Building of the Presbyterian Church
7 B.B.C.

The importance of Belfast with Newtownabbey is shown by the large proportion of the people of Northern Ireland who live in or near it. The joint population of the city itself is 420 196 out of the total of 1 536 065 in 1971. It is to Northern Ireland what London is to England but perhaps more so as it has no rival large cities such as Birmingham and Manchester. Not only is it the capital city, containing the Government Buildings at Stormont (Fig. 79) and many other offices, but it is the largest port (Fig. 80), the greatest industrial city, the headquarters of commerce and banking, the cultural and educational centre, the focus of all main communications by road, rail, sea and air (Fig. 81), the centre of the legal system and the busiest shopping centre in Northern Ireland. Its influence spreads over the whole country in a multitude of ways. Even most of the country's bread is baked in the city whilst its newspapers circulate throughout the Province.

The Port

Belfast is by far the largest port in Northern Ireland both in respect of the area of its docks and in the trade which passes through them. It has 73 berths and 8 miles (12.9 km) of quays

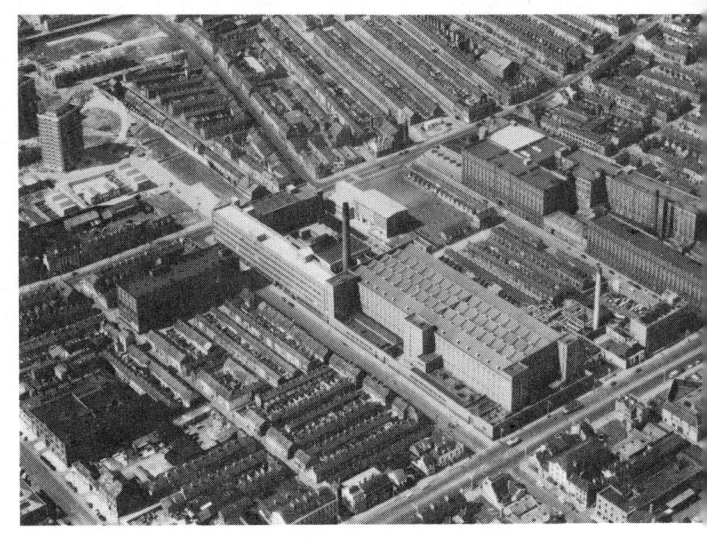

76. Western Industrial Area, aerial view, showing factories and terrace housing

with a depth of 30 ft (9.2 m) at low water. Twenty-five acres (10 ha) are covered with transit sheds and the largest of some 70 cranes can lift 200 tons (203 metric tons).

In 1971, 6506 ships entered the port with a total tonnage of 7 millions (7.2 million metric tons) and carrying about 6½ million tons (6.6 million metric tons) of freight. The port

77. Pollock Dock and a large flour mill

78. Aerial view of Belfast looking north, showing industrial expansion of the city

was modernised in 1956/7 to keep pace with its growth and more recent improvements allow for container and ferry services. A large dry dock has been added to the facilities for building and repairing ships (Fig. 82), whilst extensive aircraft, oil refining, flour milling and fertiliser plants occupy large areas of low-lying lands which have recently been reclaimed from the sea.

Daily passenger, vehicle ferry and cargo services are maintained to Liverpool and regular freight services to Holyhead, Southampton, Garston, Rotterdam and other west European ports. Container ferry services have been introduced and vehicle ferries are operating to Liverpool, Heysham and Ardrossan. Container tonnage is about 1.9 million tons (1.9 million metric tons) a year. There are over 100 container and ferry sailings per week.

79. Government Building at Stormont

80. Aerial view of the port of Belfast

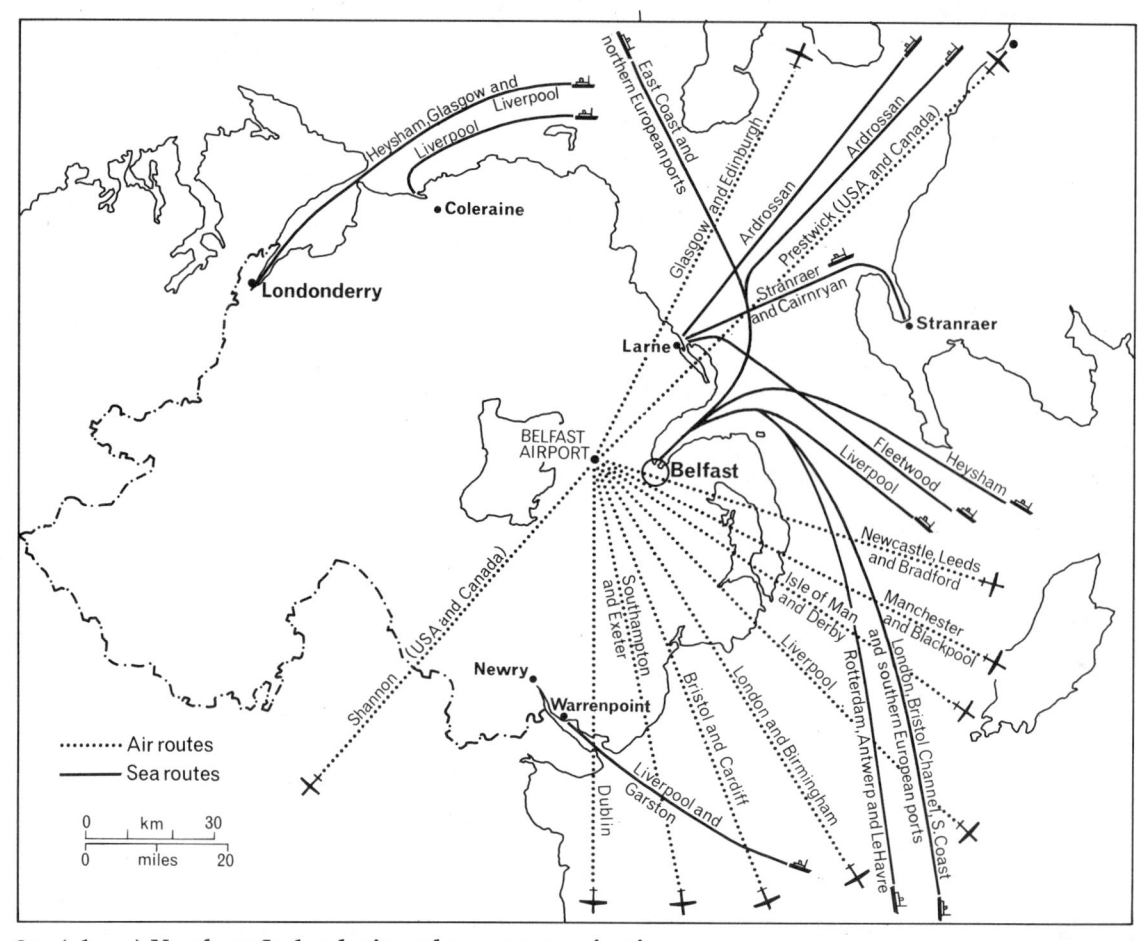

81. (above) Northern Ireland, air and sea communications

82. (below) New dry dock in Belfast

Industry

In Fig. 83 the major industries of Belfast are shown. Nearly half the companies are engaged in textiles and clothing (Fig. 84) which cover a very wide range of products. Both natural and artificial fibres are used in the manufacture of many types of cloth and of ropes, sacks and nets. Large quantities of fancy goods including embroidery are produced. There is a long-developed skill especially amongst the women in all these industries. Engineering industries include ships and aircraft, textile machinery, castings, pumps, and electrical goods. Food industries are represented by the processing of local farm produce such as bacon, lard and butter as well as by the production of mineral waters, whiskey, flour and meals, baking and confectionery and tobacco. Some 30 different industries are found in the city.

The City Centre

The picture (Fig. 75) shows clearly the straight, wide streets and general rectangular pattern which forms Central Belfast. Located within its garden and dominated by its domed structure is Belfast City Hall which stands in the heart of this area, Donegal Square. Large shops and offices surround the perimeter of this central square. Just to the north, with Donegal Place – Royal Avenue as its main artery, lies the major commercial and shopping centre. The district to the south of the city contained in the last century the city premises and warehouses of the linen manufacturers but today it is much more diversified in its use with industrial showrooms, the offices of the B.B.C. and the Ulster Bus Co.'s central headquarters. A half mile (800 m) to the west is the central bus station as well as two famous educational establishments – The Royal Belfast Academical Institution and the College of Technology. To the east are Central Railway Station and the quays and docks of the port.

Whilst many of the nineteenth century buildings have been adapted to modern purposes, much new construction is taking place and large modern blocks of offices and shops are slowly changing the appearance of this central area.

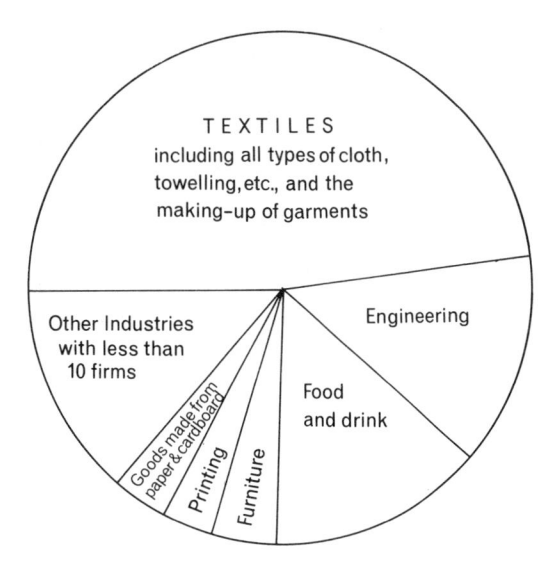

(Each industry is represented as a percentage of the total number of firms engaged)

83. The main industries of Belfast

84. Textile industry: clipping and baling sisal and manila

The Belfast area

The towns and the country surrounding Belfast abound with evidence of the influence of the city. Major roads converge through this surrounding area from all directions to make use of the Lagan valley from the west and the

51

south, the Glengormley gap from the north and the Dundonald gap from the east. There are also the coastal routes on both sides of the Belfast Lough from Carrickfergus on the north and Bangor on the south. The great importance of the Lagan valley is emphasised by the construction of the first motorway to the west (Fig. 85).

Industries with their main focus in Belfast have spread to the surrounding towns: flax spinning and weaving, for example, have been important at Hilden and Lisburn from the days of the Huguenot, Louis Crommelin. More recently man-made fibre factories have been established at Carrickfergus and Kilroot, whilst older linen and bleach mills, some now closed, are widespread near the many streams. Lime-free water from the basalt plateau in South Antrim has always played an important part in locating the linen industry in this area.

The use of the land by farmers reflects the demands of the city market. Dairy farms are frequent and widespread in the Lagan valley and neighbouring parts of Co. Antrim. Most farms along the shores of Strangford Lough and on the slopes of the Hollywood Hills provide some horticultural produce whilst nurserymen find a ready sale for their plants, roses and shrubs. Soft fruits, especially strawberries and raspberries, are locally of importance at Maze some ten miles (16 km) up the Lagan valley from Belfast.

It is within this wider area that the citizens of Belfast must find their recreation for Belfast is a closely built city with only limited open spaces. Bangor, the seaside resort on the south coast of Belfast Lough, is the second largest town in the area. Cave Hill has become a countryside park and zoo. Many golf courses are to be found whilst sports grounds for football, cricket, hockey and tennis occur in most centres. Yachting clubs have their centres both in Belfast and Strangford Loughs. At Balmoral just within the city boundaries are the show grounds of the Royal Ulster Agricultural Society, which form the centre for many other activities.

The bus frequency map (Fig. 86) shows how the influence of Belfast is felt throughout this area. The density of traffic increases markedly at Lisburn, Antrim, Dromore, Ballynahinch, Newtownards, Bangor and Carrickfergus. This group of towns lies near the fringes of the commuter zone which is linked to the city by very strong trading and commercial ties. Within this zone urban expansion and influence bear upon every aspect of life, but especially in the spread of housing and in the extent to which public services are provided. The farthest of these towns is 17 miles (27 km) away, a fact which is some measure of the size of the Belfast area. The physical features are the key to the shape of the expansion pattern. People have flooded over the lowlands and the coastal areas, leaving the South Antrim Hills (Divis Mt 1500′, 457 m) and the Holywood and Castlereagh Hills comparatively free. Only through the gaps at Andersonstown and Glengormley has the urban population penetrated into the former and in the Dundonald gap into the latter. Urban settlement spreads along the Lagan valley to Lisburn, engulfing Finaghy, Dunmurry and Lambeg on the way, along the coast to Carrickfergus, including Whitehouse, Whiteabbey, Jordanstown and Greenisland,

85. **The M1 Motorway, the first in N. Ireland. It follows the valley of the river Lagan to Lisburn and provides a major route to the west and south**

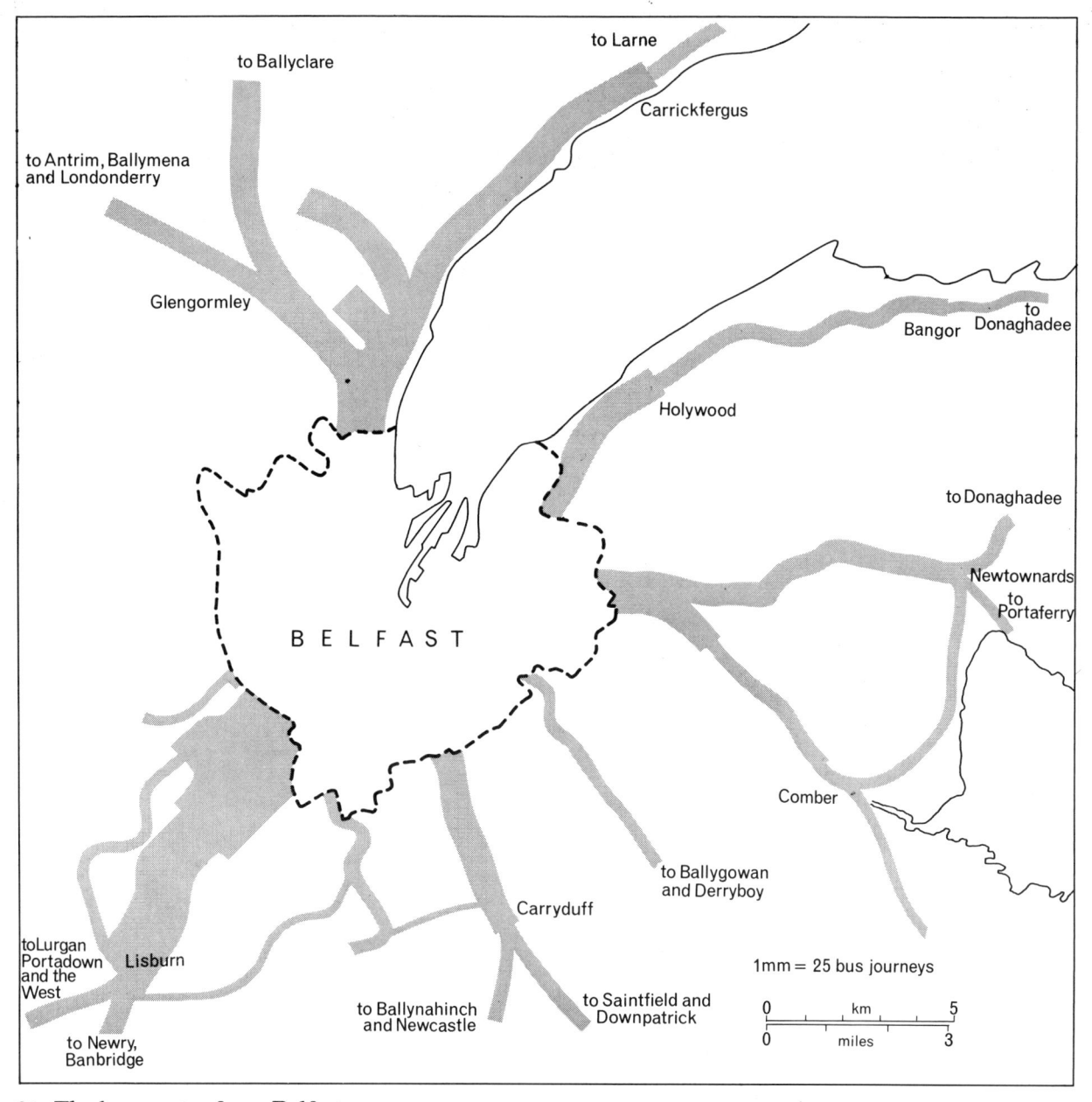

86. The bus-routes from Belfast

and similarly with intervening smaller settlements to Bangor on the south coast of Belfast Lough. It has pushed through the Dundonald gap as far as Newtownards. This bursting outwards of the population in the present day had its parallel in the nineteenth century when such areas as the 'Parks' of the Lisburn Road and the mansions of Fitzwilliam Park were built. It is another period of rapid growth in the population of the city.

Education and culture

Belfast stands out as the chief educational and cultural centre of Northern Ireland. It has the largest and until fairly recently the only university, which provides a very wide range of courses in all major faculties. Its College of Technology works closely with the university and is linked intimately with the industrial needs of the city, especially in engineering. The Colleges of Education – Stranmillis and St Mary's – are large and provide a variety of courses for teachers whilst its schools have fame far beyond the limits of the Province.

There are many scientific and cultural societies; its museum reflects the history and culture of the whole province; theatrical, musical and sporting events all add to the richness of city life. Its churches, notably St Anne's (Church of Ireland) Cathedral, the Presbyterian Assembly and St Patrick's Cathedral (Roman Catholic) reflect the strong and varied religious life of the city.

Questions on Colour Map D

1. Make a sketch-map to show the docks and the channels at the mouth of the river Lagan. Compare this with the picture (Fig. 80) which shows the port of Belfast.

2. Draw a sketch-map to show the geographical position of Belfast. Upon it insert:
   (a) the outline of Belfast Lough;
   (b) the river Lagan, Blackstaff and Forth;
   (c) the 300 ft contour. Shade all land over 300 ft;
   (d) name Cave Hill, Divis and Braniel Hill;
   (e) the chief gaps through the surrounding hills, and
   (f) the main roads which use them.

3. Study your maps and the pictures in the text and write a paragraph stating how the physical geography has influenced the position of Belfast.

8 INDUSTRIES - OLD AND NEW

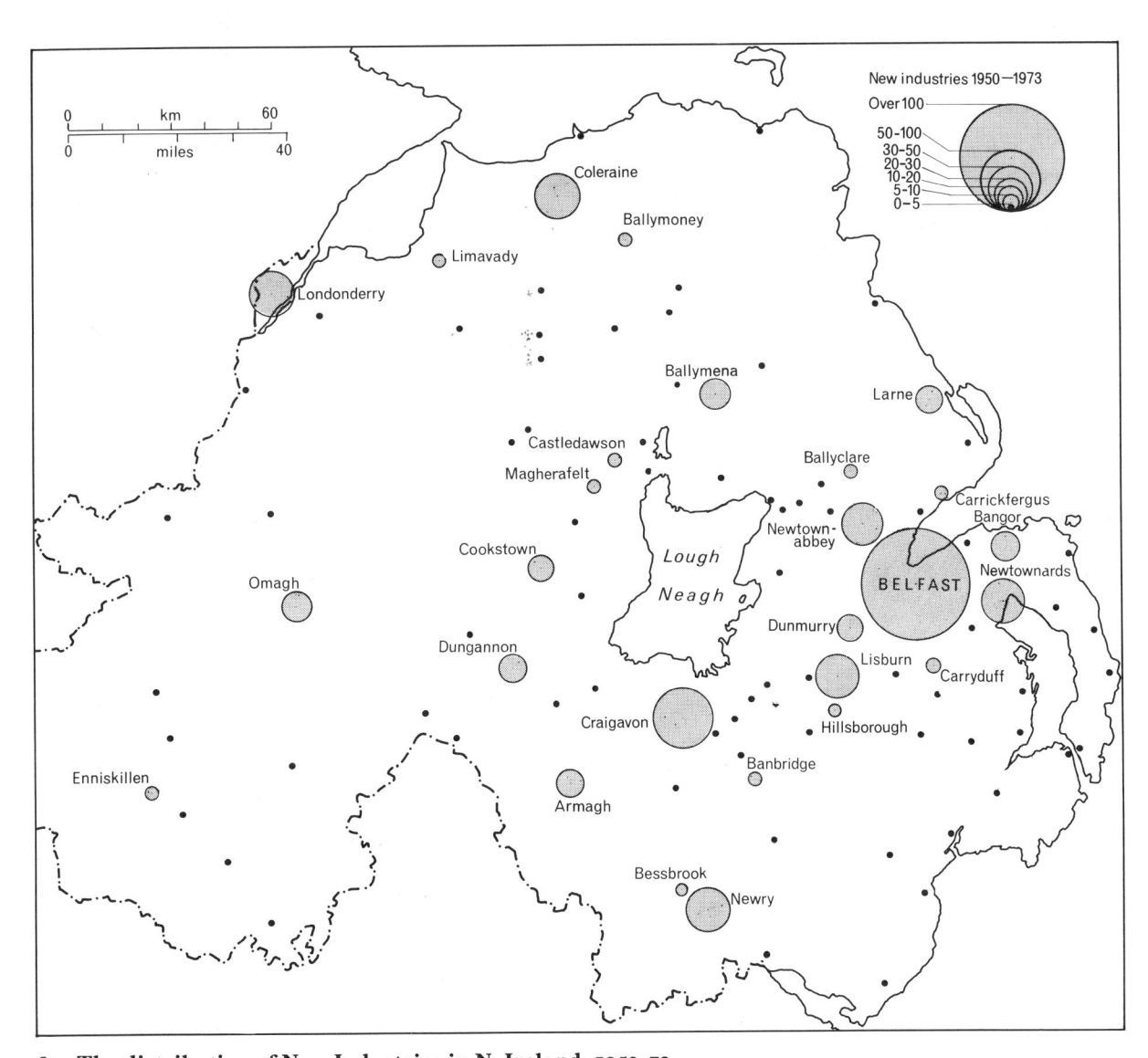

87. The distribution of New Industries in N. Ireland, 1950-73

The industrial landscape (Fig. 87)
Northern Ireland has difficulty in providing enough employment for its people, especially the men. In 1975 unemployment amongst men was 9.4% of the working population and that of women 6.0%.

During the nineteenth century more industry grew up in the North than in most parts of Ireland. Most of this industry was situated near the ports, especially around Belfast. In fact it was only in Belfast that a large urban-

55

dwelling population developed; elsewhere the factories were spread thinly in the smaller towns or along the side of a stream with a cluster of houses nearby.

Nineteenth century industry was concerned mainly with shipbuilding and linen manufacture. For the former there were no local raw materials but an excellent site for shipbuilding existed on the low-lying lands surrounding the upper shores of Belfast Lough where the river Lagan enters the sea. It was this sheltered site, easily accessible to sources for the supply of iron, steel and coal from Great Britain, which made it possible for the industry to grow. Today, with world-wide competition, it is often difficult to maintain enough ships under construction to keep all the berths full.

At first a number of small yards occupied the site but over the last half-century these have been replaced by one large shipyard. Many famous ships, both merchantmen and naval craft, have been built; amongst these are the liners *Canberra*, *Amazon* and *Pretoria Castle*, as well as many cargo ships, tankers, bulk carriers and cross-channel ferries.

Modernisation has been taking place in the shipyards to enable the very large modern tankers and bulk carriers to be built. A large dry dock (Fig. 82) has been built and a new building yard by the Musgrave Channel is

88. A drilling rig built in Belfast for use in marine investigations for oil

taking shape. The dry dock is 250 ft (76 m) across and will be the largest in the world. New to the shipyards is the building of drilling rigs (Fig. 88). Shipbuilding has led to the growth of many other industries which make parts and fitments for ships. Engineering has become important; so has rope and cable making and the manufacture of ship's furniture. Shipbuilding is a heavy industry and most of the workers are men. Unfortunately it has been a contracting industry and the number of men employed has fallen in recent years. The industry employs workers with a wide range of skills, from designers, draughtsmen and mathematicians to platers, joiners, electricians, welders, etc., so many-sided is the work of building a ship.

Linen is an industry which from domestic beginnings grew into a large factory industry during the last century. More recently it has had to compete with cloth made from many other fibres, natural and man-made. Up to 1950 much of the flax was grown in Northern Ireland. Many derelict flax dams and scutch mills testify to its widespread importance. Most farmers grew a few acres wherever the land was suitable. Today flax growing has almost ceased (only 20 acres (8 ha) was recorded in both 1962 and 1963 and no mention is made in the *Ulster Year Book* for 1972). The raw material is imported from the Low Countries and the Baltic areas of the U.S.S.R. The majority of the mills engaged in linen-making lie within 25 miles (40 km) of Belfast. In most of the towns around and also in west Belfast the red-brick mill with its tall chimney is a landmark, but with the contraction of the industry many of them are either closed or are used for other purposes.

The industry still maintains a high standard of quality, making not only traditional materials such as damasks but newer ones like suitings for both men and women. For many years flax has been used with cotton but now it is also combined with rayon and other man-made fibres in a wide range of new textile materials.

These two older industries, shipbuilding and linen, have formed the core of industrial life in Northern Ireland; the latter has left an imprint in the landscape of many towns in the presence of the large mill surrounded by a cluster of small terrace houses in which the workers lived. But two major industries form a very narrow base upon which to support the industrial life of the country and often in periods of recession high unemployment and much hardship have occurred. Indeed, even with the introduction of many new industries these difficulties have not been fully overcome.

Since the end of the Second World War in 1945 great efforts, supported by the Government of Northern Ireland, have been made to widen the industrial base by the introduction of further industries; so much so that in fact Northern Ireland has undergone a considerable industrial revolution (Fig. 87). Most of these newer industries have been established within 30 miles (48 km) of Belfast but some have grown up further afield (Fig. 89). The only industries which could use local raw materials were those connected with agricultural products – such as milk and potato processing and meat packing, and those making specialist articles from wool such as suitings and carpets.

The aim has been to introduce new industries which require a considerable amount of skilled labour. Companies in such industries may at the outset have to bring with them a limited number of skilled operatives but they tend in time to become dependent on local labour trained by themselves. Because of high unemployment, they find the recruitment of good labour easier than in most parts of the United Kingdom. Once established they tend to develop roots in the locality and prosper despite the disadvantages of distance from major markets and the sea crossing. The most important groups have tended to make use of the skills already developed in the linen and shipbuilding industries.

All the major synthetic fibres – rayon, nylon, terylene, polypropylene and polythene – are made in the province. At Carrickfergus, near Londonderry and near Antrim large new factories have been built (Fig. 90). With their well-kept lawns and flower-beds and their open, well-planned construction, they blend into the open countryside. So far, not enough industries to use the products of these factories exist in Northern Ireland and much yarn must be exported. Knitwear, especially ladies hose, dress and shirt materials, and carpets all provide local outlets for the yarn.

Engineering has long been an important industry in Northern Ireland. Such firms as Davidson and Mackie enjoy world-wide fame for pumps and other engineering products, but here the base of activity has now been widened especially in the field of electrical engineering. Great alternators, computers, telephone cables and switch gears are amongst the products made. Although there is no motor assembly plant in the Province, components such as distributors, alternators, exhaust systems and batteries are all produced in a number of smaller but usually well-equipped and well-sited modern factories in the industrial estates (Fig. 91).

Two other groups of industries must be mentioned. One is based upon older industries but the other is entirely new. Clothing and footwear manufacture have long been established. Shirtmaking has been a major industry for a long time especially in Londonderry, but recent developments have extended the industry into dress-making and tailoring. Stocking and general knitwear industries have also grown up in more than one centre (e.g. at

89. A large new factory near Londonderry, overlooking Lough Foyle

90. Aerial view of a synthetic fibre factory near Carrickfergus

Dundonald and Enniskillen). Boot and shoe making by Lotus at Banbridge and Tuffs at Ballymena have provided a further expansion of footwear manufacturing.

The second of the new groups of industry began with the opening of an oil refinery on the shores of Belfast Lough by B.P. The plant has a large level site just to the south of the deep water channel in Belfast Lough so allowing the tankers to draw alongside to unload. This may well prove to be a growing point for a number of subsidiary industries.

Tobacco and cigarette manufacture have long been established but recent expansions by Gallaghers include a large new factory in Belfast and another just outside Ballymena. Carreras have also built a new factory near Carrickfergus.

The map (Fig. 87) shows the widespread character of the post-war growth of industry

91. An industrial estate near Dunmurry

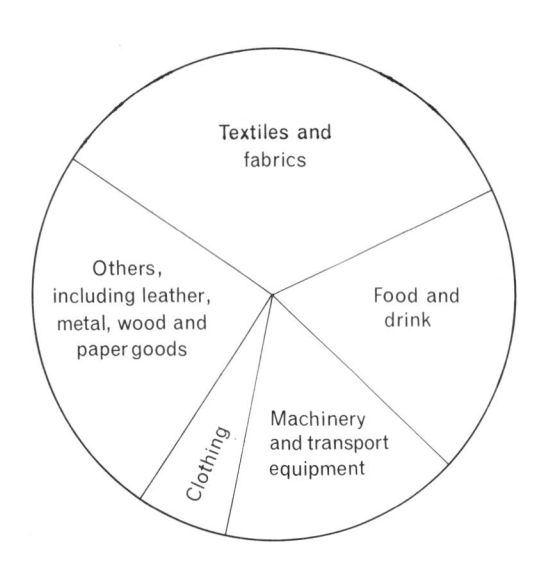

92. Exports of manufactured goods from N. Ireland (percentage of total value) 1974

and the diagram (Fig. 92) the manufactured products which are exported. Northern Ireland has become less dependent upon a few industries and agriculture. Industry must always suffer from distance from its markets in Great Britain and from the sea crossing between them but the position of Northern Ireland near the sea provides an easy link with overseas countries. It also lacks many raw materials. In fact all its major industries, except food processing, depend upon imported raw materials. Yet in many processes, especially in tyre making and textile manufacture, its adequate supplies of fresh water are vital.

To prosper, Northern Ireland must make relatively valuable products, not too heavy or bulky in relation to their value, so as to offset the freight charges. The special measures taken by the Government of Northern Ireland in the acquisition of sites and in the building of factories aids the establishment of industries whilst at present there is an ample source of workers upon which the new industries can draw.

Questions on the map of New Industries (Fig. 87)

Make a tracing of the map of Northern Ireland and then do the following exercises.

1. With its centre at the head of Belfast Lough, draw a circle on a radius equal to that from Belfast Lough to Larne. Estimate the number of new industries within the circle and write the number in it.

2. Repeat exercise 1 using the same radius and taking Craigavon as the centre.

3. For any other centre with five or more industries draw a circle around it of half an inch diameter. In each circle write the number of industries.

4. Count the industries outside the circles you have drawn and write:
   (a) the number west of Lough Neagh,
   (b) the number east of Lough Neagh.

5. What do the answers to the exercises 1–4 tell you about the distribution of new industries in Northern Ireland?

9 FARMING

93. Discussing the use of the land

Farming (Fig. 93) is one of the most important occupations in Northern Ireland, although the number of people employed in it tends to become less. Formerly farming was of a mixed type, with crops and livestock on every holding but there is an increasing specialisation on livestock and their products. Mechanisation has greatly increased, so reducing the need for hand labour. Over 36 000 tractors are used on the 40 000 farming units whilst 37 500 farms have mains electricity which enables many types of machine (e.g. milking machines) to be powered. Farms are becoming larger by the amalgamation of small farms into larger units.

(Between 1966 and 1971 the number of farms fell by about 2½ per cent per annum.) This allows the more economical use of machinery and often permits the use of larger machines such as combine harvesters. Such large machines are often hired for specific purposes.

The ownership of agricultural land has for many years been a most important aspect of farming. As a result of a long series of Acts of Parliament between 1870 and 1925, most farms now belong to the farmer who works them. Some 17 000 of the farms are very small, less than 30 acres (12 ha), and do not provide an adequate living for the farmer and his family but there are about 18 000 farms with an area of between 50 and 70 acres (20–28 ha) and a small number are even larger. These farms are generally large enough to provide an adequate income to support the farmer and his family and to permit modern farming methods to be used. A system of letting, called conacre, is widespread and accounts for about 19 per cent of the farm land. Originally it was a means of letting small areas of land for a short period, usually 11 months, to landless farm workers for growing small crops of grain and potatoes for their own use. With the purchase of land through the Land Acts, it became the only legal means of letting land whilst annuity payments were being made, but it has continued after these were completed. It enables elderly owners, widows, and others who do not farm or who have a very small holding to let their land for short terms without having to sell it. Often the land is let by auction to the highest bidder although many personal agreements are made. Many small, uneconomical holdings are let in this way and the land included in bigger farm units.

The end product of the farms is usually livestock. Crops are grown largely for fodder although most land is used for grass. Excluding some 600 000 acres (240 000 ha) of rough grazing land which is often in mountainous areas, rather less than two million acres (or 400 000 ha) are used for crops and grassland – or 80 per cent of the total land area. Of the total land under crops in 1966 barley occupied nearly 50 per cent of the cropped area, oats 25 per cent and potatoes 16 per cent. By 1975 there were considerable changes – barley 66 per cent, oats 12 per cent and potatoes 14 per cent (Fig. 94).

The usually mild climate, with rainfall spread over the whole year, is most suitable for the growth of grass. The spring is the driest season and provides conditions suitable for ploughing and sowing but late summer is often wet and makes harvesting of corn crops and the making of hay difficult. 'Saving the hay' is a common local expression full of meaning. The number of farm animals has increased over the years since 1950 and by 1975 the numbers of cattle, pigs and sheep were 1 626 000, 645 000, and 934 000 respectively. Poultry for egg production or table use are found on most farms, sometimes on free range but often reared by intensive methods such as deep litter. Frequently they are the responsibility of the farmer's wife, who takes the profits. There were in 1975 12 million chickens together with some 96 000 turkeys and about 24 000 ducks and geese. Turkeys, ducks and geese have tended to decrease in numbers.

Much of the produce is exported, mainly to Great Britain, and amounted in 1974 to £187 millions or about 14 per cent of the total exports. The table, from the *Ulster Year Book*, 1976, gives the details (Fig. 95).

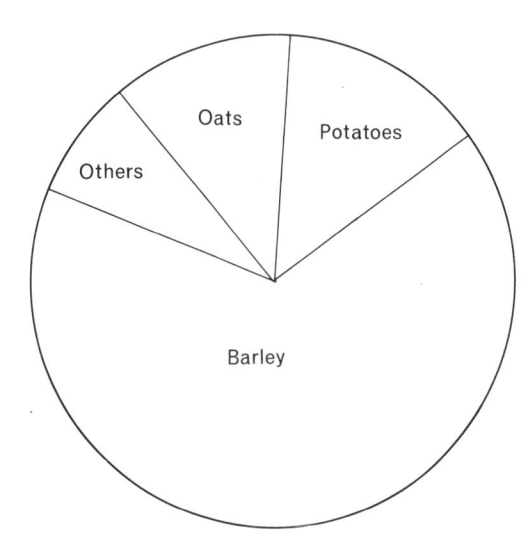

94. Percentage of arable land in N. Ireland occupied by different crops – 1974

95. Livestock and other animal and vegetable products exported (percentage of total value) 1974

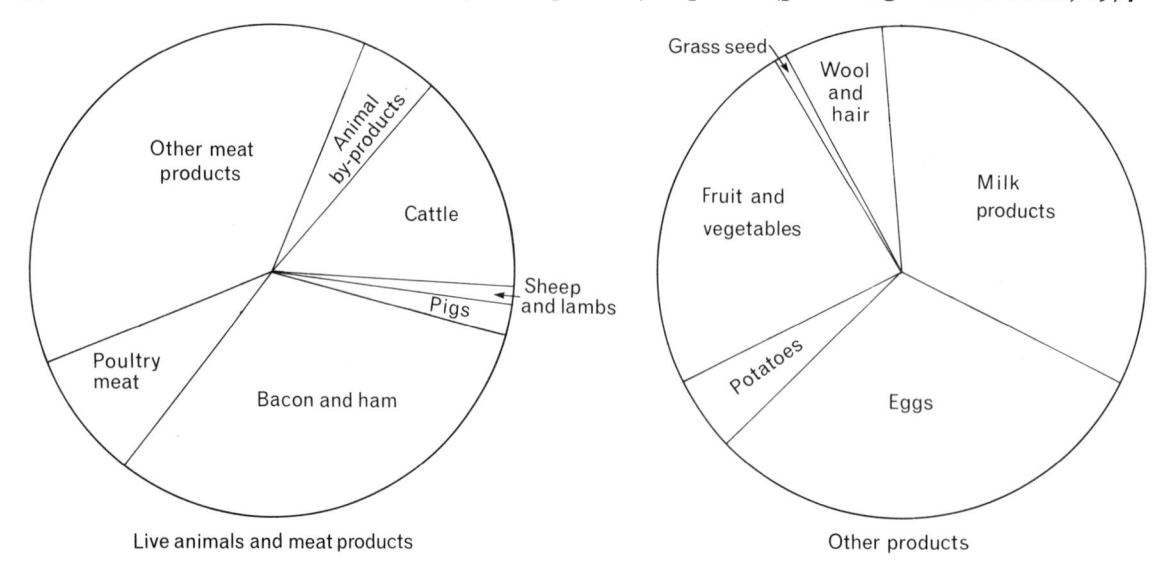

Live animals and meat products

Other products

£ (thousands)
Live animals and meat products exported

cattle	15 114
sheep and lambs	913
pigs	1 954
bacon and ham	31 339
poultry meat	8 020
other meat products	37 664
animal by-products	7 052

£ (thousands)
Other products exported

milk products	28 314
eggs	24 656
potatoes	3 875
fruit and vegetables	20 548
grass seed	132
wool and hair	6 296

Selling these large quantities of produce from many small farms has led to the development of centralised marketing arrangements usually by government-sponsored agencies. Each commodity has its own special scheme but the purpose of them all is the same: (i) to organise selling to large manufacturing and distributing firms at fair prices, and (ii) to guarantee the standard of quality of all produce sold. Many of the schemes came into existence as long ago as 1930 to combat the slump in trade but they have been changed and strengthened to meet the needs of trading at the present time.

Farming forms a very large industry, affecting directly some 11 per cent of the people and many more in supporting industries. The farms differ considerably one from the other in making the best use of the physical conditions of relief, climate and soil and in satisfying the needs and interests of the farmers. Some descriptions of different farms follow. They are not only in different parts of the country but they also have their own particular characteristics.

Farm 3 (Fig. 96)

This farm is situated in the middle of the drumlin country of Co. Down. It is owned by the farmer and contains land, (i) upon the drumlins where the soil is well-drained but clayey in character, (ii) in the valleys and hollows between the drumlins where the drainage is poor, and (iii) on the solid slaty rocks where the soil is thin and the rocks often come to the surface. The farm is about 200 ft (61 m) above sea-level and has an undulating relief. The maps (Fig. 96) show the position of the farm buildings and the fields which make up the farm. As in most Irish farms, these are small (1–3 acres, 0.4–1.2 ha). Each field has its own name and these not only give an intimate picture of the character and location of each but show how closely the farmer is linked to his land. Many of the names give a glimpse of the history of the land use. The use of the fields changes with the rotation of crops but for 1966 it is shown in the table below:

Field	Crop
C, D and K	barley
O	ploughed to be sown with grass
A	orchard
B, E, F, J, P, M, N and L	grass

(From the table and the map, work out the percentages of the area of the farm used in each way).

The stock includes 10 milking cows, 740 pigs, 100 poultry, 70 sheep and 30 beef cattle. (Devise a chart to represent the stocking.)

The farm is mechanised with two tractors, harvesting and other machinery and has a mains supply of electricity which powers the static machinery including the milking machines. All the work on the farm is done by the farmer and his family.

Farm 4 (Fig. 97)

This is a coastal farm on the low, flat shorelands of Strangford Lough (Fig. 98). The alluvial or sandy soils are light and easy to work. The farm lies in the rain-shadow of Scrabo Hill to the west which protects it from the strong and generally cold north-west wind. It is situated in one of the driest parts of Northern Ireland with a rainfall of less than 30 inches (76 cm) per annum. The farm is engaged in vegetable growing for the large urban markets of Belfast and Bangor.

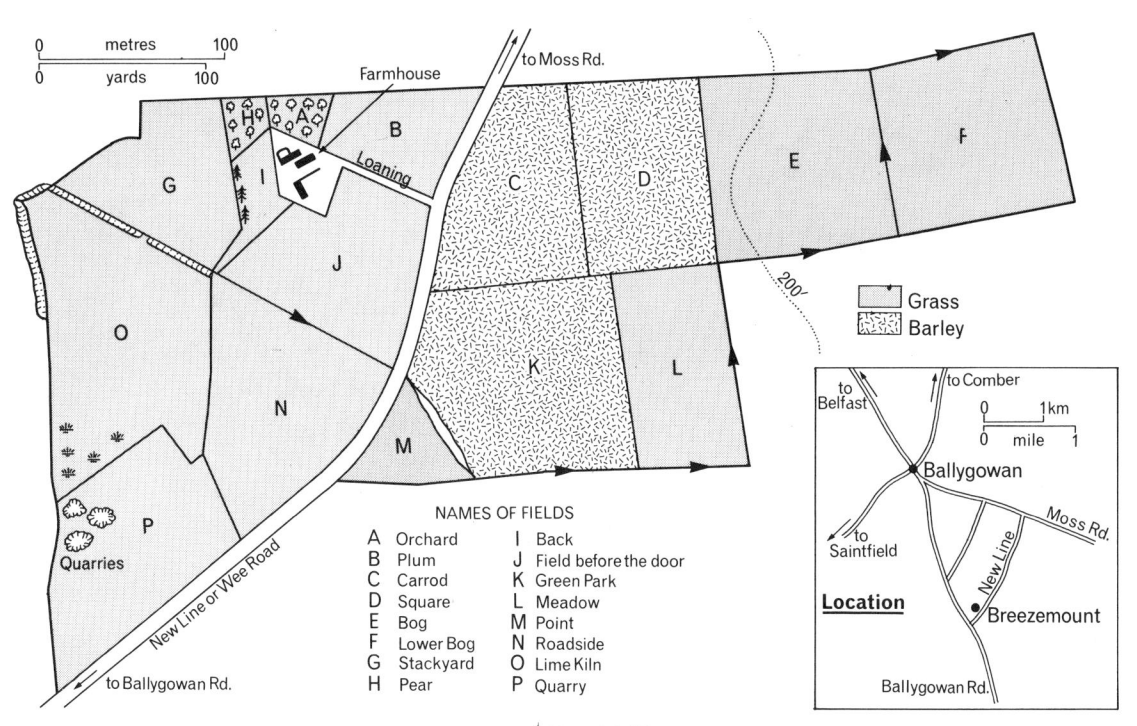

96. Farm 3: A lowland mixed livestock farm in mid-Down

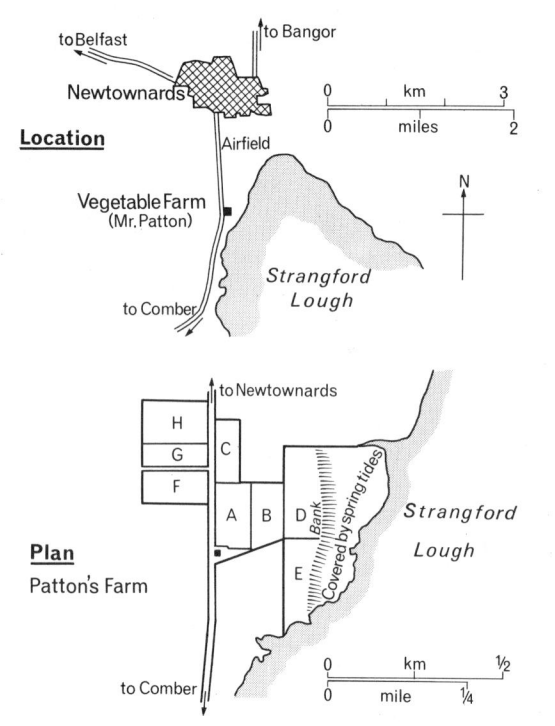

97. Farm 4: A small specialist vegetable farm on the shore of Strangford Lough

The maps (Fig. 97) show its location and its fields. In all it contains about 30 acres (12 ha) of which 13 acres (5.2 ha) are within the tidal limits of Strangford Lough and useless for cropping. Three fields H, G and F are rented in conacre. There are no animals on the farm but it is fully mechanised and has a packing plant to prepare the vegetables for market.

In 1968 the fields were being used as follows: A, C and G were in vegetables – carrots, parsnips, brussel sprouts, cabbage and leeks – crops which find a ready sale and are widely used by Irish families. Fields B, D and E were being used for hay whilst F was in grass and let for grazing. A sowing of grass for a season or two gives the land a rest from intensive vegetable growing. There are also 100 hens in deep litter kept on the farm.

The farmer employs two full-time men throughout the year and as many as twelve casual workers for weeding during the summer months. The casual workers come from the nearby town of Newtownards. All the produce is purchased by merchants in Newtownards

98. Farm 4, looking towards Scrabo Hill

99. Farm 5: A dairy farm in the Lagan valley

and transported by lorry to market in Belfast, some ten miles (16 km) away.

Farm 5 (Fig. 99)

This farm lies south-west of Belfast near Dunmurry. The farmhouse and farmyard lie on a small hill, an outcrop of Bunter Sandstone, and the fields spread out around it (Fig. 99). The soils vary considerably from fairly light loams on the hill slopes surrounding the farmyard to some fairly heavy clay soils at lower levels. The total area is 90 acres (36.4 ha) but the farmer works two other holdings with it, one in the Lagan valley of 300 acres (121.4 ha) and the other of 130 acres (52.6 ha) on nearby Colin Mt. This makes a total holding of 520 acres (210.4 ha), a very large farm for Northern Ireland.

Lying within 4 miles (6.4 km) of Belfast, the farm is mostly engaged in supplying milk to the city. The centre of the farm activities is a pedigree herd of some 30 Ayrshire cows. Ten young heifers are kept as future replacements of the dairy cows. An Ayrshire bull is kept so that it is unnecessary to purchase stock from outside the farm. The cows produce 2500 gallons (11 361 litres) of milk per month which are sold to the Milk Marketing Board. The main herd is kept on the Home Farm but the young stock are grazed at the second holding in the Lagan valley.

A subsidiary enterprise – beef cattle raising – has been developed on the upland grazing on Colin Mt. Some 40 Aberdeen Angus cows are kept to suckle the calves. There is also an Aberdeen Angus bull. The calves are not fattened but sold when they are six months old. The mountain pasture is not rich enough to fatten them.

In addition to these major enterprises the farmer keeps 25–30 ewes which utilise the grass rejected by the cows, 50–60 pigs and a few poultry. Much of the land is used to provide grazing and other food for the livestock.

About 50–60 tons (51–61 metric tons) of hay and 200–300 tons (203–305 metric tons) of silage are fed to the cattle. High protein meals are purchased for the dairy herd whilst 25–30 tons (25.4–30.5 metric tons) of barley are grown for the mountain beef cattle and the pigs.

To work this large farm the farmer employs two full-time men and is helped by his wife and son.

Farm 6 (Fig. 100)
This farm lies near the north coast of Co. Antrim and consists of two holdings about 10 miles (16 km) apart; one is 700 acres (283.3 ha) but includes some peat bog and forest, and the other is 160 acres (64.8 ha) of which 30 acres (12.1 ha) are peat bog (Fig. 100). The farm lies on the slopes of the Antrim plateau and the soils, based upon the glacial drifts, vary from light soils on the Antrim moraine to much heavier soils on the boulder clay. The farm is fully mechanised with 3 tractors, 2 combine harvesters, a rotovator, ploughs, sugar beet and potato planters and reaping machines, together with grain silos and corn grinders. There are nine men employed.

The main enterprise is pig-rearing – mainly Yorkshire Whites and Landrace. Some 1000 pigs are kept, varying from newly-born piglets to breeding sows. Two boars are kept. Subsidiary to the pig-rearing are turkey production and a herd of 100–130 Hereford cattle for beef production. Between 200 and 300 hens are kept.

Tillage is mainly concerned with the production of 160 acres of barley which is used as pig-food. There are 20 acres (8 ha) of sugar beet, an experimental crop which is refined in the Republic of Ireland. Thirty acres (12.1 ha) of potatoes are sold through a local wholesaler. The remainder of the land is under ley grass for grazing cattle and the making of silage and hay.

Farm 7 (Fig. 101)
The farm is situated in the far west of Northern Ireland, a few miles east of Strabane in Co. Tyrone. It lies on the eastern side of the valley of the river Foyle. The country is hilly and the farm forms a long strip farm stretching down the hillside from an altitude of 425 ft (135.6 m) down to 70 ft O.D. (21.3 m). The total area is 51 acres (20.6 ha) plus 18 acres (7.2 ha) rented in conacre. The farthest field is more than a mile from the farmstead. The soils are based upon glacial drifts and river gravels, the former tending to produce heavy clay soils and the latter lighter-medium loams with some gravelly patches.

Until relatively recently, the farm formed part of a larger unit of 110 acres (44.5 ha) which was worked by the present owner and his brother. However marriage caused the holding to be divided. Fragmentation of this kind is less common than amalgamation but the example shows how closely farm ownership is linked with the personal life of the farmer.

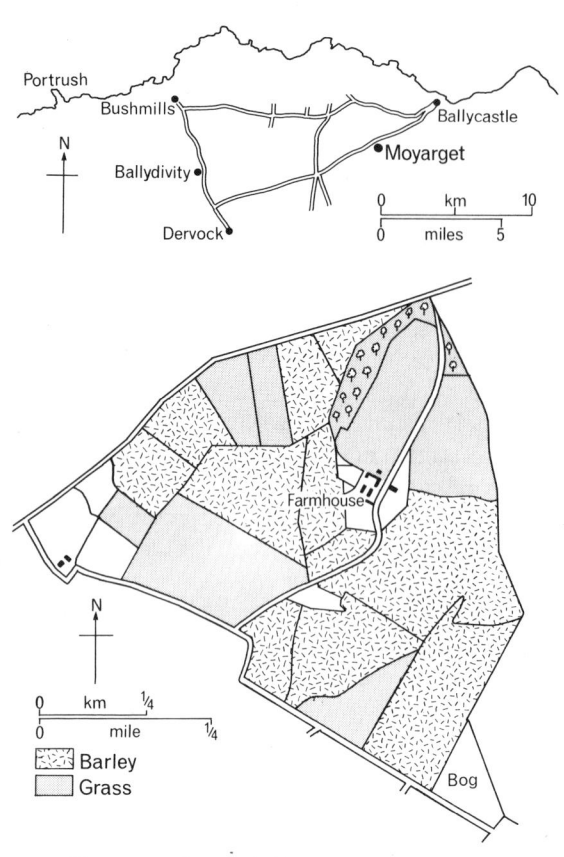

100. Farm 6: A specialist pig farm in north Antrim

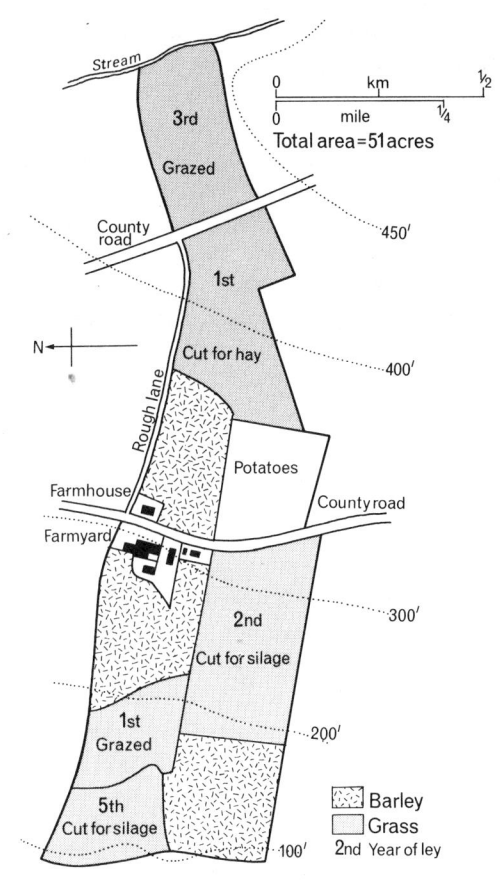

101. Farm 7: A mixed livestock farm in Tyrone

The basis of the farm economy is livestock. A herd of 12 Aberdeen Angus cows is kept to suckle their calves. The latter are fattened and sold into the baby beef market at 14 months. Another 20 Shorthorn/Aberdeen Angus crossbred stores, at about two to three years old, are bought in the spring and a similar number in the autumn for fattening and sale in the local market. Twenty border Leicester/Suffolk crossbred ewes are kept and average 1½ lambs each, producing a flock of 30 lambs which are sold to dealers from France. Pig production was started in 1966 and has now expanded to 15 sows – Landrace/white Yorkshire crossbred. The young pigs are fattened and sold for bacon.

Provision of food for this livestock forms the backbone of land usage on this farm. Between 12 and 20 acres (5–8 ha) of barley yielding 30 cwts (52 kg) to the acre are grown. Twenty acres (8 ha) are in grass from which 200 tons (203 metric tons) of silage are made and in a dry year 6 acres (2.4 ha) of this are used for hay. The only crop not directly related to the livestock, is 5 acres (2 ha) of potatoes, usually an early variety, which is sold either for table use or seed. To maintain this programme of tillage 20 tons (20.3 metric tons) of fertilisers are used whilst to keep up the protein content of animal food 3 cwts (152 kg) of animal concentrate are purchased and mixed with each ton of barley.

Although the farm is now run as a separate unit, the two brothers co-operate in the ownership of machinery and in the employment of one man. This enables the farm to be well-mechanised with tractor, harvester, muckspreader, seed drill, potato planter and digger – in fact all the major machines needed to run such an enterprise.

Advantage has been taken of government grants to renew the buildings which are less than six years old. These include silage pots, two cattle courts and collecting yards, a pig and general-purpose house. Fencing and land drainage works have been undertaken. It is now a thoroughly modern farm. With only one shared worker the farmer and his family must undertake the major part of the work, an arrangement which is typical of the livestock family farm.

Farm 8 (Fig. 102)

This is a hill sheep farm lying high on the Antrim Hills mostly over 1000 ft (304.8 m) and in places as high as 1500 ft (457.2 m). Much of the land is mixed heather moor with hill grasses, rushes and moss. The original holding was 1000 acres (404.7 ha) but now increased to 1400 acres (566.6 ha). The land is of low fertility and includes only 6 acres (2.4 ha) which are cropped. The basis of the farm economy consists of 420 black-face mountain ewes. In addition some hardy Galloway cattle are grazed in the summer months. The ewes are wintered in lambing pens on the farm instead of the more usual practice of wintering in the lowlands. This farmer prefers to winter

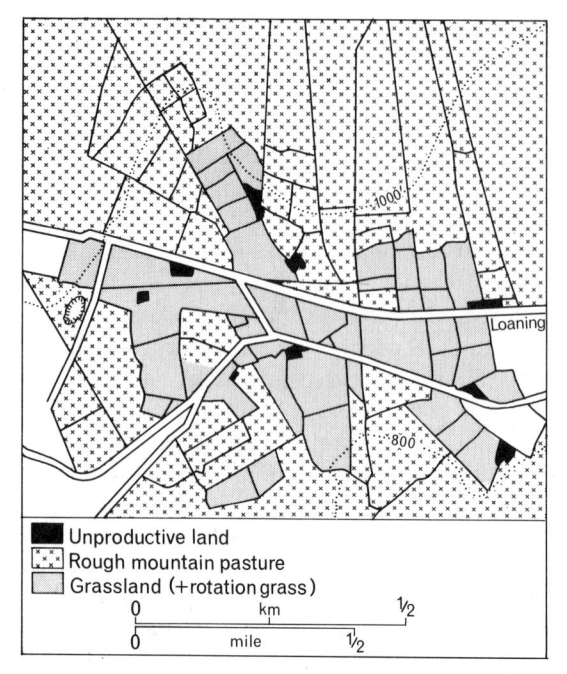

102. Farm 8: A hill sheep farm in the Antrim hills

his own flock and considers that lambs make better progress when they can make full use of the new herbage in the spring. It also avoids the expense of hiring lowland grazing.

The rams are bought in Scotland, usually at Newtown Stewart. The farmer favours the Galloway type of black-face which has a lighter fleece and stands up to the hard moorland conditions very well. Usually black-face ewes produce one lamb a year and the farmer considers it a bad year if he does not rear 90 per cent of the possible lambs, i.e. about 400 lambs a year. Most of these are sold as stores for fattening on richer lowland pastures.

Life on a highland farm is remote and lonely – a long loaning being its only connection with the main road system. The climate is severe and hard frost and much snow must be expected in the winter. Precipitation (including snow) is high – 60 or more inches (152.5 cm) per year. The only workers on the farm are the farmer, his wife, his son and his daughter. It is solely a family enterprise except that neighbouring farmers share the work of clipping, dipping and marking the sheep. This custom of aiding one another at busy seasons is very common and goes far back in history; it is often called 'neighbouring'. It may become less common as farming becomes more specialised and more commercial in its purpose.

These six farms illustrate some aspects of farming in Northern Ireland. Between them they show some of the variety of Northern Ireland farming: farm 3 – a lowland mixed livestock farm; farm 4 – a small specialist vegetable farm; farm 5 – a mainly dairy farm of large size on the fringes of Belfast; farm 6 – a large specialist pig farm; farm 7 – a mixed livestock farm in the far west; farm 8 – a very large hill sheep farm. Study other farms and note how they compare with those which are mentioned here. There are still other types of farms such as hill cattle farms, very large-scale dairy farms, fruit or fruit and cattle farms and large-scale poultry farms.

Local customs and local methods abound in farming. Some still persist, whilst others have tended to die out as modern mechanised methods have been introduced. As old methods are replaced the tools which were used fall into disuse and yet enough remain to enable the observant student to see much of the history of farming. Farming, once a way of life providing the farmer with his own simple needs, has now become part of the commercial world, striving for greater production to meet the needs of large urban and industrial populations. Much of interest is contained in Professor E. Estyn Evans's book *Irish Heritage* whilst a visit to the Ulster Folk Museum at Cultra near Bangor is well worthwhile.

10 | THE PEOPLE - THEIR ORIGINS AND CUSTOMS

Northern Ireland, composed of the six north-eastern counties of Ireland – Antrim, Down, Londonderry, Armagh, Tyrone and Fermanagh – came into existence just over 50 years ago as a partly self-governing State within the United Kingdom. Yet it forms part of the old Irish Province of Ulster which also included Donegal, Cavan and Monaghan, counties now forming part of the Republic of Ireland. The physical geography of Ulster differs considerably from the country to the south. It is only here and there that the limestone rocks of the Central Plain of Ireland penetrate northwards across the border where the rocks are schists, grits, and volcanic materials. The border country between Ulster and the rest of Ireland was in many places originally very wet and boggy so that only at the seaward ends near Sligo and Dundalk were there dry causeways crossing it. Where weaknesses occurred in the natural barrier they were made good in those remoter times by the Black Pig's Dyke – a series of defensive works. Thus Ulster stands apart physically and in many ways has nurtured a different human story from the rest of Ireland.

This north-eastern part of Ireland was occupied by man as early as 6000 B.C. Along the coast of Antrim the tools of these fishermen can be found, made from the flints which occur in the chalk rocks. These same fishermen penetrated inland to Lough Neagh to tap the rich supplies of fish there. By 3000 B.C. men of the New Stone Age (Neolithic) were beginning to settle in the uplands and bring with them early farming methods. The countryside is rich in remains, especially burial cairns and tools, particularly of the period 2500–1500 B.C. They speak of a flourishing culture whose distinctive character separates Ulster from the rest of Ireland. Trading, especially along the sea-lanes between Ireland, Great Britain and Brittany, was a feature of this period.

These early farmers found most of the land covered with forest and many clearings must have been made to provide land for pastures and corn. The clearing of the land of trees and boulders led to a long and continuous struggle against the natural conditions; one fought with varying success. As part of it, livestock, notably cattle, became a mainstay of the farming and have remained so ever since. Many of the present-day customs find their origins back in these early times. Superstitions relating to cattle are common and plants such as the whitehorn are looked upon as symbols of luck or ill-omen. Family ties were always very strong and kinship still remains one of the strongest bonds in the community. The farm-cluster until recent times was the commonest settlement pattern and housed a family community. The infield–outfield system of cultivation has been replaced by the dispersed family farm standing in its own land. The rural village with its community life did not develop and urban communities came to Northern Ireland as recently as the seventeenth century.

It seems likely that the earliest settlers, who came as life became possible after the Great Ice Age, remained undisturbed by invaders until the years just before the birth of Christ. At this point in time, Celtic-speaking peoples came to all parts of Ireland, bringing with them the Celtic language and its tradition of learning and poetry. They probably enslaved the native population but they also accepted many of the customs connected with the pastoral farming which had taken root. To Ulster, peoples came from Scotland whereas to the south of Ireland they came from southern Britain or Europe. The Celtic folk-tales tell of conflict between these two peoples who came from such different places. It seems likely, too, that the Celtic saints, who spread Christianity, followed different routes and established different spheres of missionary influence, centring round the work of Bishop Palladius in the south and that of St Patrick in the north. The Church, adopting much Celtic custom, became monastic in its organisation. During this same period the expanding Roman Empire never reached Ireland. Later the Norsemen came but they established no lasting settlement in Ulster whilst the Anglo-Normans fared little better, being confined to the coast. Thus the influence of these last two invaders seems to have been less in Ulster than elsewhere in Ireland.

The next important stage in the peopling of Ulster came in the seventeenth century. Conflict had broken out between England and Ireland in the reign of Henry VIII but it was not until late in the reign of Elizabeth I that a vital stage was reached in Ulster. Resistance was strong in this part of Ireland and consequently Ulster was subdued and 'planted' (i.e. colonised) by English and Scottish settlers. This plantation was more thorough in the north-east and thinned out towards the southern and western boundaries of Ulster. Not only did this bring new communities into Ulster, but it occurred at the time when the Reformation had led to the establishment of Protestantism (Presbyterianism in Scotland and the Church of England in England) and thus arose a religious division between the original population who had remained Roman Catholic and the Planters.

This division remains strong today despite the fact that for two and a half centuries the two groups have lived together and in many material ways have shared a common tradition. The Celtic festivals such as Halloween (31 October) are observed by both groups. They share the same dialects of English in different parts of the Province and these all contain an intermingling of words and expressions of Celtic origin. They share the same dry, satirical humour and many of the same folk-beliefs. Place names have usually remained Celtic whilst the townland – the oldest division of the land into kin units – remains in all areas with some of its old legal and social importance. Both share the same regional house types and use the Ulster spade which differs from other Irish spades in having a hand-grip. Later they shared in the concentration in Ulster of the domestic linen industry – using home-grown flax – as a part-time occupation shared with farming. From this root there grew in the nineteenth century the factory industry which has distinguished Ulster from the rest of Ireland. In all these ways and many others both groups have been involved, but there has also been long-standing isolationism and suspicion. From time to time hostility has overflowed into violence, with serious loss of life and destruction of property. Yet it is also true that large areas have remained peaceful with those of different political and religious views living calmly side by side.

The twentieth century has seen the partition of Ireland into Northern Ireland and the Republic of Ireland. Although the majority of the people of Northern Ireland wish it to remain a part of the United Kingdom others would like to see the whole of Ireland become a single state independent of Great Britain. So mixed indeed are these two communities that no boundary could be devised which would group together those of like mind without causing the uprooting and migration of families who have lived in a particular area for many generations. In fact at the time of Partition the old county boundaries, which simply follow rivers and streams and paid no heed to loyalties or beliefs, were used.

Despite these conflicts the Ulsterman has his own strong regional personality, which distinguishes him as much in Ireland as it does in Great Britain. He has a rooted resistance to change which is such a strong characteristic of our times. His resistance preserves many valuable qualities in him but it allows many old ways to remain. Professor Estyn Evans depicts him so aptly: 'At his best the Ulsterman of whatever religious background, combines realism with idealism and action with contemplation. The shadow of the stockman strides behind him, reluctant to praise, given to negative affirmations. He has a rough surface and the robust home-spun quality of Ulster linen. He cannot disown his Irish heritage. (*Transactions of the Institute of British Geographers*, no. 51, p. 17).